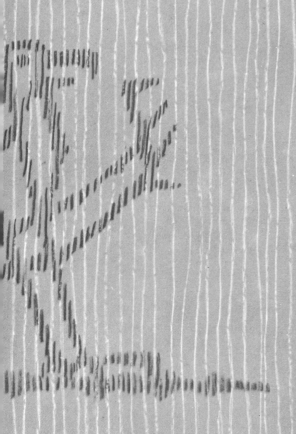

SPECIAL CONSULTANTS

THE GOLDEN TREASURY OF
KNOWLEDGE

VOLUME
5

OF SIXTEEN VOLUMES CONTAINING 420 BASIC
ARTICLES WITH 2500 ILLUSTRATIONS AND MAPS

Margaret Bevans
EDITOR-IN-CHIEF

Joanna Aldendorff
EDITORIAL CONSULTANT

Clifford Junceau
PROJECT CONSULTANT

Tom Torre Bevans
DIRECTOR

EDITORIAL STAFF
Renée Algrant · Doris Ballard · Richard Keigwin
I. W. Klein · Morgan Larkin · Henry Mins
Carol Z. Rothkopf · Peter Share

PRODUCTION STAFF
Rosalie Barrow · Frank Bologna · Ken Braren
Rosemary Gutwillig · Alan M. Heicklen
Yvonne Charles Johnson · Harris Lewine · Alice Lupo
Peter Marks · Tomaso Puliofito · Bruce Ross · Loretta Trezzo

COVER BY Ned Seidler

GOLDEN PRESS · NEW YORK

About VOLUME 5 and how it relates to other volumes

Open this volume anywhere, and you will find an article to inform and interest you. Any article you read will make you want to increase your knowledge by reading more about that subject or about related subjects. And there are fascinating facts and accounts throughout all the 16 volumes of *The Golden Treasury of Knowledge*. Just use the index in Volume 16, and you will be guided to further reading.

If THE WRIGHT BROTHERS has made you curious about the origins of flight, you will want to read about the experiments of LEONARDO DA VINCI. NEW ZEALAND may lead you to read about CAPTAIN COOK, or THE ANTARCTIC, or GEYSERS. HORSES will interest you in ASSES, and PHARMACY will lead to THE WONDER DRUGS. PLANT CELLS is a natural beginning for inquiry into CHLOROPHYLL, the green coloring matter of plants. TURTLES will make you wonder about PREHISTORIC REPTILES.

Just as there are related articles, there are related subjects in other articles. The reindeer herding of THE LAPPS may interest you in THE DEER FAMILY, and JOAN OF ARC in FRANCE. So don't stop reading. With the help of the index in Volume 16, store up all the knowledge you can absorb.

© 1958, 1959, 1960 by Fratelli Fabbri Editori, Milan, Italy and published by special arrangement with them.
Copyright © 1961 by Golden Press, Inc. Designed by Bevans, Marks & Barrow, Inc. Printed in the U.S.A. by Western Printing and Lithographing Company.
Published by Golden Press, Inc., Rockefeller Center, New York 20, New York. Library of Congress Catalog Card Number: 61-10594.

CON

TENTS

See page 445 for a time chart which will show how periods of history relate to one another and at what time many of the events in these articles took place.

The Lapps

The Lapps do not have a country of their own. They live in the northern regions of four countries: Norway, Sweden, Finland, and the U.S.S.R. These northern regions are called Lapland. Lapland is about 150,000 square miles in area, which makes it a little larger than the state of New Mexico.

More than half of Lapland is within the Arctic Circle, and temperatures are low all year round. In summer the average temperature is only about 57 degrees Fahrenheit. During the winter there are long periods when the temperature is below zero. In the northern part of Lapland there is constant daylight in summer and constant darkness in winter.

The western coast of Lapland is Norway. It has many fiords, narrow inlets of the ocean between high, rocky cliffs. Farther east there are many lakes and swamps. In summer the swampland is infested with mosquitoes.

Little farming is done in Lapland because of the cold weather. However, there is an excellent mineral supply. Lapland's copper mines and iron deposits are among the largest in the world. There are also many forests of pine, fir, spruce, and birch trees.

The Lapps probably came to Lapland before the birth of Christ. Because the country produced so little in the way of fruits and vegetables, the ancient Lapps lived by hunting and fishing. There are fish of many kinds in the rivers and lakes. Trout, perch, pike, salmon, cod, herring, and halibut are in abundance.

The northern regions of Norway, Sweden, Finland, and Russia are known as Lapland.

In spring, nomadic Lapps try to find new pastures for their herds of reindeer. They will travel as many as 100 miles to find suitable pasture land.

Huts made of wood or stones covered with earth are used when the Lapps stay for a long time.

Two ancient carved wooden figures which were probably meant to represent Lapp gods.

During winter, nomadic Lapps live in huts made of wood. These huts have no windows. A fire is usually built inside for warmth.

Long ago, the Lapps learned that reindeer were so important to them that they could mean the difference between life and death. Reindeer live easily in the cold climate and eat the wild plants and moss that grow in Lapland. Reindeer give milk and meat. Their skins can be used for clothes and tents. Their horns and bones can be made into tools, and reindeer tendons can be used to make thread. The Lapps learned to domesticate reindeer, and now the chief business of Lapland is reindeer herding.

A Lapp market in spring is often filled with color-fully dressed men and women who have come to buy or exchange goods. The different kinds of hats are all Lappish. Probably the most interesting is the Cap of the Four Winds, at right. It has four points: three are stuffed with straw so that the hat can be used as a pillow. The fourth corner is empty and used as a wallet. The material most used for bowls, dishes, and jugs is wood, which is often beautifully carved.

There are over 350,000 reindeer and only about 30,000 Lapps.

In former times, Lapps moved a great deal, looking for better pastures for their reindeer or for better fishing grounds. Because they moved so much, Lapps were called a nomadic people. Most Lapps today are not nomads. They have found it convenient to have permanent homes.

There are still some nomadic Lapps, how-ever, who never build permanent homes. For shelter in summer the nomadic Lapps live in tents made from reindeer skins. In winter they build shelters of tree branches. When the weather is not too cold they live in huts made of stones or wood covered with earth.

The Lapps are considered Mongolians. Their hair is dark and hardly ever turns gray. They have high cheekbones and rather flat noses. Lapps are usually less than five feet tall.

Even though the Lapps are isolated, the world has learned from them. The Lapps are believed to have invented skis. They were the first people to domesticate reindeer. In the field of art the Swedes have been greatly influenced by the Lapps, and many designs which we con-sider Swedish came originally from Lapland.

The Wright brothers made their living from their bicycle shop. But their first love was airplanes, and they worked at night and on Sundays on plans and models.

The Wright Brothers

Beginning in the fall of 1900, the people of Kitty Hawk, North Carolina, witnessed a series of events that resulted in the beginning of the air age. Wilbur Wright and his younger brother, Orville, of Dayton, Ohio, began to spend many hours on the sand dunes and small hills along the North Carolina coast studying the motions of their large and complicated kites. Since about 1895, when the brothers had read about the experiments of Otto Lilienthal, a German glider pilot, they had been fascinated with the idea of a glider that would sustain itself in flight. Every moment they could spare from business they devoted to study and experiment on flying machines.

Life in Dayton had not been easy for the Wright brothers. Their father was poor, and they left school early to go to work. They founded a newspaper, which they wrote, printed, and sold themselves. But they were more interested in mechanics, and they soon gave up the newspaper and started a bicycle factory. In their shop they also built and repaired kites and gliders.

In 1901 the brothers built a simple wind tunnel in which they tested various kinds and shapes of wings. As a result of their experiments, they built a large glider with rectangular wings. By a simple arrangement of strings, the rear edge of the wing could be curved up or

The Wright brothers got their inspiration from a German glider, constructed about 1895. By moving his arms, a man was able to make the wings of the glider move, thus sustaining himself in flight.

down. If the wind raised one wing in flight, its edge was turned up and the edge of the other wing turned down. This kept the glider balanced. Aileron control, as their discovery is now called, was essential to the progress of the science of aviation.

In the summers of 1901 and 1902 the Wright brothers again went to North Carolina to test their newest kites and gliders. They made a glider that could carry a man. One of the brothers would lie flat on the lower wing. The other would push the glider down the slope of a sand dune. Then, as the wind caught the wings, the glider would float for a few yards to a safe landing. More than 2,000 tests of this sort were made, and the brothers became expert glider pilots.

Now they needed a motor to keep the glider in flight. This was not a simple matter. Nowadays it is known that motors must produce at least one horsepower for each pound of weight, but in those days no one knew how to build such an engine. The brothers built the lightest engine they could, but it weighed 250 pounds and produced only 12 horsepower. They hoped that this would be enough to make their first airplane fly.

The next problem was the propeller. The

brothers read everything they could about ship propellers. Then they began a series of experiments and discovered that a single propeller tended to turn the flying machine in the opposite direction from the propeller's rotation. They decided to use two propellers turning in opposite directions. They attached them to their new machine and christened it the *Flyer*. But no one knew yet whether it would really fly.

Late in 1903 the Wrights distributed an announcement in the towns around Kitty Hawk that they were prepared to fly their machine. The date selected for the attempt was December 17. Not more than four or five people took the announcement seriously, and the first flight of a motor-powered plane had a tiny audience.

The plane was drawn from a shed the brothers had built on the hill and set up facing the wind. Orville crawled out onto the lower wing. In his right hand was the gas lever and in his left the rudder control. Cords controlling the slope of the wing tips were attached to his body.

Wilbur twirled the propellers, and Orville moved the throttle forward. The machine vibrated and shook. Its skids began to move along a rail that had been built on the ground. Wilbur ran along, pushing the wing with his hands. The plane rose a few inches above the ground,

At Kitty Hawk, North Carolina, on December 17, 1903, the Wright brothers made the first successful motor-powered flight. Only a few people came out to watch this historic event.

then rapidly climbed to a height of several yards. The machine covered only about 125 feet in 12 seconds, and then came to rest. The motor was too heavy for the power it produced, but the first airplane *had* flown.

The Wrights made several successful flights that day and decided to devote all their time to flying. They founded a company to build and test their machines, and they made improvements in their motors. On October 5, 1905, Wilbur flew for 38 minutes over a small circular course, covering a distance of 24 miles, and the next year the brothers took out a patent for their invention.

In 1908 Wilbur Wright went to Europe, where he attracted world-wide attention with flights covering greater and greater distances. He received many medals and honors for his pioneering work.

Orville concentrated on proving to the American government that the flying machine worked. In 1908, for the first time, he remained in the air more than an hour. In 1909 he made many longer flights, and the government accepted the new machine. Although the brothers sold the Wright Company to other investors, they continued to be vitally interested in the airplane industry. After Wilbur's death in 1912, Orville went on studying and experimenting. He died in 1948.

The Wright brothers were among the great American inventors and pioneers. Their invention has done as much to change the world as anything discovered in our century.

Wilbur Wright, the older of the two brothers, was born in 1867. His death from typhoid fever in 1912 was a great loss to aviation.

Aristotle

Aristotle and his teacher, Plato, were two of the greatest thinkers of the ancient world. Aristotle was born in Stagira, Thrace, in 384 B.C. His father was a doctor. When he was 17 years old Aristotle went to Athens, Greece, in order to study at Plato's school in the Academy there. Although Aristotle started at the school as one of Plato's pupils, he soon began to work with Plato as a fellow teacher and to help him with his scientific research.

Aristotle wanted to find the answers to many questions about natural history. He was not satisfied with the answers other men had found. Most people believed that the things we know today about plants and animals were caused by magic. And Aristotle did not believe in magical powers. He thought that his questions could be answered only if he studied science. He was especially interested in biology— the study of animal life. And his amazing intelligence led him to make many discoveries.

Aristotle stayed at Plato's school for 20 years. During those years he and Plato never really disagreed about anything important. But when Plato died, Aristotle decided to leave the school. He spent some time at Assus where he studied with some other former pupils of Plato. Then he moved to the island of Lesbos so that he could study the animal life of the sea.

In 342 B.C., Aristotle was invited to Macedon by King Philip II. The king wanted Aristotle to teach his 14-year-old son, Alexander. Aristotle taught Alexander for seven years. When King Philip was killed, Alexander became King of Macedon. He started out to conquer the Persian Empire. Alexander became known as Alexander the Great and he was much too preoccupied with war to take time to study. So Aristotle returned to Athens. But all his life Alexander sent specimens back to Aristotle for study.

In Athens, Aristotle set up his own school. The school came to be called the Peripatetic School. The word peripatetic comes from the

Aristotle taught his pupils as they walked in the garden of his school.

Greek word which means to walk. Aristotle and his pupils often walked and talked in the garden of the school. Aristotle gave lectures to his pupils. He taught them about history and politics and philosophy. He told them about how the animals of land and sea live and grow. And he helped them find the answers to their own questions by means of logic. Logic is the science of finding the truth by thinking and reasoning.

Aristotle often wrote down his lectures and these writings have been kept through the years. Today it is possible to go to a library and find a copy of Aristotle's lectures to read. He also wrote down his ideas while he was studying with Plato. One of his last works was a large encyclopedia.

Toward the end of his life, Aristotle was forced to leave Athens. No one doubted his great intelligence or his ability as a teacher. But he had once taught Alexander the Great, and he had been one of Alexander's friends for many years. Alexander had made enemies among the people he conquered. Among these enemies in Greece were men who did not want a friend of Alexander's to teach the young men

A marble statue of Aristotle

of Athens. So they made Aristotle leave his school. He went to his mother's home in Chalcis. Here he died in 322 B.C. at the age of 62.

For many centuries after his death the teachings of Aristotle were considered the only true answers to questions of science, philosophy, and politics. His teachings were so long considered perfect that they hampered scientific research. Aristotle's thinking had been so advanced for his time that people forgot it was no longer modern more than a thousand years later. Now modern science has disproved many of Aristotle's ideas, but Aristotle was one of the greatest thinkers of all time.

Fireflies—Living Lanterns

Fireflies are beetles. They are also called glowworms and lightning bugs. But none of these names is accurate, for fireflies are neither flies, nor worms, nor bugs, and they have nothing to do with fire or lightning. Glowworms are true fireflies and may be either wingless females, or the young, wormlike larva. Both forms give light.

These unusual insects belong to several families of beetles, and they have always fascinated people. In the West Indies and South America they have been worn as hair ornaments, put in cages, and·used as house lights and outdoor lanterns. There are poems about fireflies and a well-known song, "Glowworm," has been written about them.

One of the many surprising things about the firefly is its signal system. Its light starts flashing every evening just after sundown, but it makes no light in the daytime. The signal is sent by the male as a mating call, and is answered by the female.

When the signals begin, the summer darkness seems filled with millions of drifting

In order to create light in an electric bulb, we must create a great deal of heat. Since all we want is the light, most of the electrical energy is wasted.

sparks. But if you catch a firefly in your hand, you will feel no heat. This cold glow of the insect is a heatless form of light, unlike any man has been able to invent.

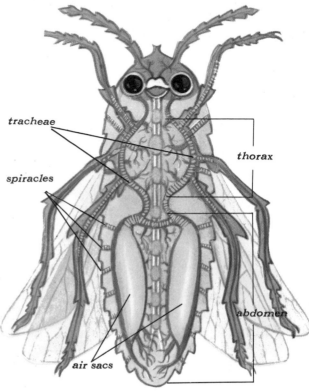

Air enters the firefly's body through small holes—spiracles. From these it passes through air tubes—tracheae—to airsacs in the abdomen.

The scientific name for such light is bioluminescence. It means creation of light by living things. A more common name is cold light, but this does not really mean cold. It means that there is no heat as there is in an electric light made by man.

When an electric lamp is turned on, the bulb soon becomes very hot. A great deal of electrical energy is being used to make heat instead of light. The firefly, on the other hand, wastes no energy. Its little power plant produces nearly 100 percent cold light.

Scientists and engineers are trying to produce cold light. We now have fluorescent tubes

Male

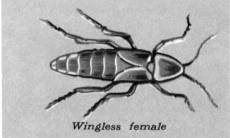

Wingless female

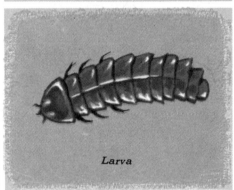

Larva

Signaling female

which give less heat and better light than bulbs. But even this light is not the equal of the firefly's. In trying to find a way to produce cold light, scientists are learning a great deal about fireflies. Fireflies produce light by breathing. Insects breathe by taking in air—which is partly oxygen—through many tubes. These tubes open on the surface of the insects' thorax and abdomen, the middle and bottom parts of their bodies. When a firefly breathes, oxygen enters the outer layer of its body. The oxygen acts upon light-making cells filled with a fatty material, called luciferin. Another material, called luciferase helps speed up this action. All three working together make the firefly's light shine. This glow is made brighter by a yellow inside layer which acts as a reflector. The shining bowl behind a headlight has the same effect.

A number of other insects are luminous. Some centipedes shine and are mistaken for glowworms. The young of a South American crane fly gives light, and it is even called a glowworm, but it is not in the firefly family at all. Click beetles show spots of light, but they are not true fireflies. On the other hand, not all true fireflies give light.

Of the fireflies which give light, many show greenish-white signals. Other signals are yellow-green or reddish. One glowworm from South America sends out red light from her head and yellow-green light from the sides of her abdomen. Male fireflies are rather handsome in daylight, but the wingless female is ugly and grublike.

Firefly signals flash off and on like light-

A firefly's light is magnified by a reflector like the reflector of an automobile headlamp.

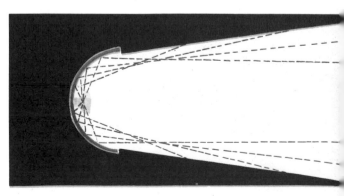

house beacons. But instead of warning, they invite. Though all the light flashes may seem the same, each kind of firefly has its own special signal. By the color and timing of the flashes, each female knows just which kind of male is calling. To answer his signals, she climbs a grass stem or twig and twists about so that her light shines upward. But she doesn't sit still. Instead, she waves her light back and forth as if she were stopping a car. You can trick fireflies with a flashlight, if you are careful to use the right light and timing. Fireflies sometimes even signal to the wrong kind of male or female, but this is rare.

Like most insects, fireflies lay eggs. When the eggs hatch, the young larvae look like worms. Because of this, there is an old and untrue story that earthworms turn into fireflies. Firefly larvae eat small insects, cutworms, and snails, and they are of great help to farmers. When they are brought indoors for study, fireflies sometimes eat raw meat, flies, and cheese.

Some adults are said to eat small insects. Others may not eat at all.

The male firefly on page 369 is less than half an inch long. It has six legs, and its wings are covered by horny sheaths. The female is wingless. In flight, the male tilts upward and lifts its hind legs well above its light. This is so that females some distance away, as well as those below him, will be able to see the signal. Males send faster signals and have better eyesight than females. Tests have shown that male fireflies send their signals about once in every two seconds. On very warm evenings the signal is faster than when it is cool. Female signals are much slower. Sometimes the intervals between the flashes are six seconds.

Firefly lamps have in the past been very useful to people who had no other kinds of lighting. And today they are showing us how to make the lamp of the future. But to most people the most important thing about fireflies is the magic they bring to a summer night.

Fireflies produce cold light by the action of oxygen on light-making cells in their bodies.

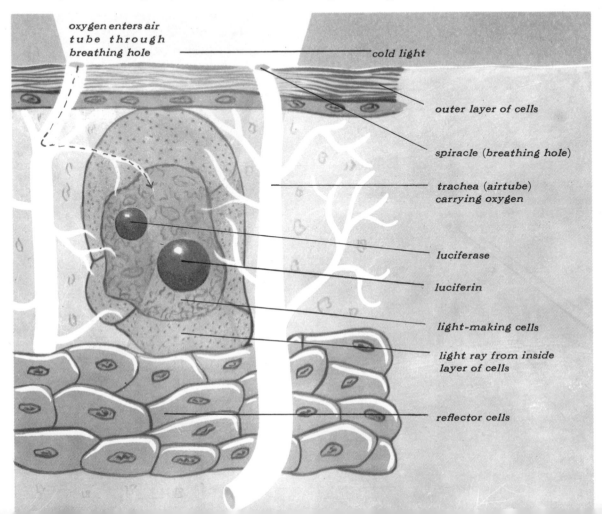

oxygen enters air tube through breathing hole

cold light

outer layer of cells

spiracle (breathing hole)

trachea (airtube) carrying oxygen

luciferase

luciferin

light-making cells

light ray from inside layer of cells

reflector cells

New Zealand

In 1642, Abel Tasman, a Dutch explorer working for the Dutch East India Company, discovered an unknown island in the Pacific Ocean. It was 1,200 miles southeast of Australia. Its high white cliffs and green landscape led him to call it Ao-tea-roa, which means Long Bright World.

This same island was discovered again by Captain Cook in 1769 when he was making a voyage around the world. Cook found that the land was an archipelago, a group of islands, more than 1,100 miles long. There were three islands, two large ones and a much smaller one at the southern end. Narrow straits separated them from one another. These, with a number of tiny islands, form the country now called New Zealand.

The islands were inhabited by a brown-skinned Polynesian people who called themselves Maoris. Their ancestors had come over the sea on rafts all the way from the eastern Pacific. The Maoris were left in peace for more than 40 years after Cook's visit, except for visits from a few explorers and some whaling ships.

The first Christian missionaries arrived in 1814, and soon settlement started in earnest. In 1841 the islands became a separate British colony. In 1907 New Zealand became a dominion of Great Britain.

A large number of Scotsmen settled on the southeast side of South Island. An English colony started on the Canterbury Plains. Now, in the south, place names are Scottish and many people speak with a Scottish accent. In the north, the names are those of English towns and cities.

With the coming of the settlers, a long and bitter series of wars began. The Maoris resented having their land taken over. The British were determined to stay. It was not until 1871 that the quarrels were settled. In the end, the Maoris kept their land, and today about 153,000 of these first New Zealanders have the same rights as the more than 2,173,000 newcomers. New Zealand is admired by many people for its liberal and democratic laws.

New Zealand covers an area that is about the size of Colorado. It has some of the most

New Zealand is on the opposite side of the globe from Europe—just as the North Pole is opposite the South Pole—and its seasons are reversed. Christmas is hot, and July is the coldest month.

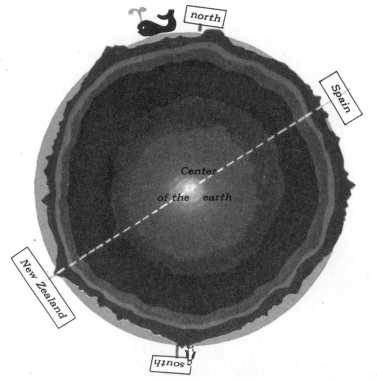

varied land of any small country. The islands are the tops of a huge undersea mountain range. North Island has active volcanoes and hot springs. South Island has glaciers and mountain peaks like those in the European Alps. In fact, the mountain range that runs along the western side of South Island is called the Southern Alps. The glaciers here are among the most beautiful in the world. Water from melting ice comes thundering down from the white peaks in marvelous falls.

On the northeastern side of the Southern Alps are the Canterbury Plains, one of the most fertile parts of New Zealand. Here are many farms and sheep and cattle ranches. Since New Zealand is in the southern hemisphere and not far from Antarctica, the weather is colder in the south than it is in the north.

Stewart Island, to the south, is lonely and beautiful. It is an island of ice covered peaks, glaciers, and huge granite cliffs 5,000 feet high. At Milford Sound, the water tumbles down over one of these cliffs in falls 2,000 feet high.

Auckland is New Zealand's largest city. It stands on a narrow isthmus with a harbor on each side. North of Auckland is a forested pen-

New Zealand is 1,200 miles southeast of Australia. There are two large and many small islands. Those place names which are not Maori words are almost entirely English and Scottish.

Auckland

NORTH ISLAND

Hamilton

Waikato

Lake Taupo

New Plymouth

▲8,270 FT. MT. EGMONT

▲9,190 FT. MT. RUAPEHU

Napier

NEW ZEALAND

Wanganui

Palmerston North

Nelson

Cook Strait

Wellington

PACIFIC OCEAN

NEW ZEALAND
AREA: *103,736 square miles*
POP: *2,315,291*
CAPITAL: *Wellington*
RELIGIONS: *Protestant, Roman Catholic, Church of England*
LANGUAGE: *English*
MONETARY UNIT: *New Zealand pound ($2.80)*

SOUTH ISLAND

SOUTHERN ALPS

CANTERBURY PLAINS

▲12,349 FT. MT. COOK

Rangitata

Christchurch

Waitaki

Timaru

Lake Te Anau

Lake Wakatipu

Lake Manapouri

Clutha

Dunedin

Foveaux Strait

Invercargill

STEWART ISLAND

PACIFIC OCEAN

insula. The enormous kauri pines grow there and elsewhere on the islands. These magnificent trees are valuable timber, probably the best softwood in the world. They also produce a yellowish resin called New Zealand varnish, and the waste is used for making paper. The trees grow 120 feet high and sometimes have trunks up to 16 feet in diameter.

The land south of Auckland has a mild and humid climate similar to the northwestern

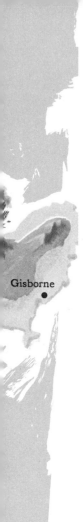

Gisborne

The kiwi lives only in New Zealand. It is almost wingless and tailless. Its feathers are like hair, it has a long, weak beak, and it hunts insects at night.

United States. This region is a plateau, rising into volcanic mountains, where there are many warm lakes and boiling springs. Occasionally jets of steam spurt 100 feet into the air like giant fountains, and small clouds of steam always hover over the landscape.

Wellington, the capital of New Zealand, is at the southern end of North Island on Cook Strait. The country's government is here and the harbor is a large and busy one.

New Zealand's climate is healthy. There is plenty of rain, wind, and sun. Most of the country stays green all year around. Seventy percent of the plants that grew in New Zealand when settlers first came could be found only in that one place. New Zealand's original animals, too, were unknown anywhere else. Except for two rare kinds of bat, the country had no mammals at all. Of course, many kinds of plants and ani-

mals have since been imported. But in some isolated places it is possible to find the hatteria, a lizard which is the only remaining member of its family of reptiles. The kiwi, a wingless bird with hair instead of feathers and a very long beak, lives only in New Zealand. Both these creatures and some of the plants are remnants of prehistoric days when the islands may have been a part of the mainland of Asia.

New Zealand's mineral resources are not great, but there is coal and oil, gold and a number of other metals. Power from the many waterfalls is cheap and plentiful. But New Zealand's main income is from sheep and cattle. It exports wool and hides, canned and dried milk, butter, and processed meat. New Zealand is the world's largest exporter of lamb and mutton, and it tops all other countries in its exports of cheese.

(Top left) Penny-farthing bicycle of the 1870's (Top right) Draisine of the early 19th century (Bottom) A modern racing bike weighs only about 14½ pounds. It is stripped of extra equipment such as brakes and fenders.

Bicycles

Bicycles are lightweight, easy to ride, and simple to repair. They enable people to travel at about 12 to 15 miles an hour, often over paths and tracks that cars and buses cannot take. Throughout the world today there are millions of bicycles in use.

The bicycle is a comparatively modern invention. For generations men built vehicles such as chariots or carts that had two wheels placed side by side. But it was a long time before a vehicle was built with one wheel in front of the other.

The pioneer step was probably first taken around 1790, at the time of the French Revolution. A primitive wooden frame was mounted on two heavy wheels, one behind the other (1). This bicycle had no brakes, no steering wheel, and no pedals. The rider moved it by pushing his feet against the ground. Since this new device was very popular with rich young men, it was known as a dandy horse.

The first practical dandy horse (2) was invented by Baron Karl Drais von Sauerbronn in 1816. He was the chief forester of the Duchy of Baden in Germany, and he found that his machine made inspection trips along forest roads much easier. This draisine—named after its inventor—added a handle bar and a saddle to the original dandy horse. The vehicle could be steered and the rider could sit down more comfortably as he pushed his way over the ground. The draisine reached England in 1818. About 19 years later a Scottish blacksmith named Kirkpatrick Macmillan produced the first bicycle with pedals and cranks to turn the wheel.

Macmillan's bicycle was clumsy and heavy, and the next important improvement was made in France. In 1855, Ernest Michaux produced a successful machine that had pedals attached to the hub of the front wheel (3). Michaux built the first bicycle factory, where 200 workers produced 140 bicycles a year.

Ten years later, another Frenchman, Pierre Lallement, introduced a heavy bicycle nicknamed the boneshaker (4). The wooden wheels had iron tires about their rims. They were stronger, but not more comfortable for riding over streets paved with cobblestones.

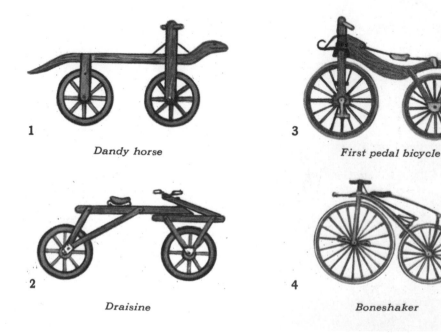

1
Dandy horse

3
First pedal bicycle

2
Draisine

4
Boneshaker

BICYCLES

The pedals on all these primitive bicycles were attached directly to the front wheel. One turn of the pedals meant one turn of the wheel. The bigger the front wheel, the farther and faster the bicycle would go as the rider pedaled. As a result, the front wheels were made larger and larger (5). In England, such bicycles were known as penny-farthings because the difference in size between the front and back wheels was like the difference in size between the English penny and the farthing. Some front wheels were more than five feet high, which made it hard to climb onto the saddle. A rider often had to lean the bicycle against a lamp post before leaping onto it. Since these bicycles still had no reliable brakes, often the only way to avoid an accident was to jump off—not an easy thing to do from such a height.

The problem was finally solved by the use of a bicycle chain (6). This chain connected the wheel of the pedals to sprockets on the axle of the rear wheel. One turn of the pedals now produced several turns of the rear wheel. Larger front wheels were no longer necessary and bicycles began to be shaped like those we know today.

The safety bicycle had a chain and two wheels of the same size (7). It was first manufactured in England, about 1885. In 1889 the Englishman John Dunlop added inflatable rubber tires, and the modern bicycle was almost complete.

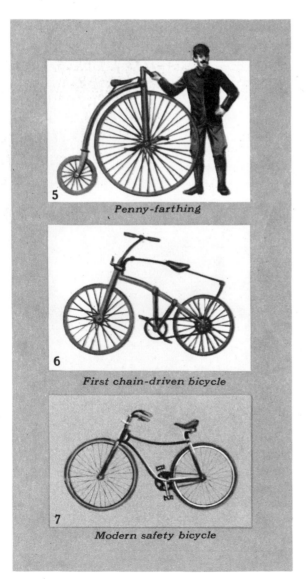

Penny-farthing (5)

First chain-driven bicycle (6)

Modern safety bicycle (7)

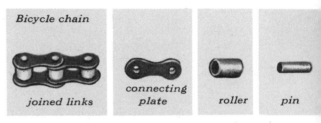

Bicycle chain

joined links   connecting plate   roller   pin

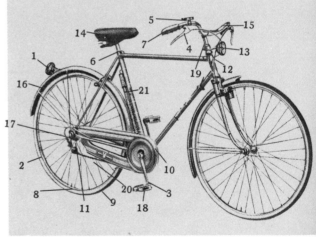

Bicycle parts

(1) *reflector* (2) *wheel rim* (3) *pedal crank* (4) *hand brakes* (5) *bell* (6) *adjustable saddle tube* (7) *hand grip* (8) *tire valve* (9) *inflatable tire* (10) *chain guard* (11) *free-wheel sprocket* (12) *brake cable* (13) *headlight* (14) *saddle* (15) *handlebars* (16) *fender* (17) *wheel hub* (18) *pedal* (19) *steering post* (20) *chain* (21) *pump*

Touring model, for a man

Sports model, for a man

Sports model, for a woman

Racing bicycle, for road races

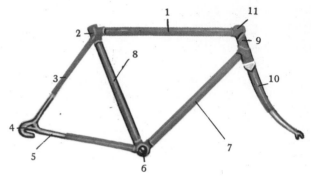

Bicycle frame
(1) *transverse tube* (2) *saddle joint* (3) *back fork*
(4) *rear axle slot* (5) *lower back fork* (6) *main
bearing* (7) *bottom tube* (8) *upright tube* (9)
steering post (10) *front fork* (11) *steering bearing*

Hollow steel frames and ball bearings were developed. A free-wheel sprocket enabled the rider to stop pedaling while the wheels continued to turn. Saddles and handle bars were made adjustable and brakes became reliable. All these improvements added to the popularity of the bicycle. In Europe hand brakes became common. In the United States coaster brakes were more popular.

The bicycle was used for sport as well as work. In the 1880's and 1890's bicycling became a craze in both Europe and the United States. Bicycle clubs sprang up, and men and women rode off into the country to enjoy themselves. Bicycle riders liked good smooth roads and it was the coming of bicycles rather than the later appearance of automobiles that brought about the earliest road improvements. The League of American Wheelmen, which was founded in 1880, was one of the leaders in the drive for better roads.

Today in the United States, bicycles have been largely replaced by automobiles. In Europe motor scooters and cars are also reducing the number of bicycles. But bicycles are still popular as touring vehicles with many vacationers. Some of the great sporting events of the world are bicycle races. The famous Tour de France and the Olympic bicycle races are still very popular. In countries such as Africa or India, where roads are rough and not many people are wealthy enough to own cars, the bicycle is a very common method of travel.

Wool

There are more than 900,000,000 sheep in the world. In Australia, which is the largest producer of wool in the world, there are about 140,000,000 sheep, although the human population is less than 10,000,000.

Sheep are raised for meat and for hides, but particularly for the wool that comes from their fleece, for wool is a wonderful textile fiber.

A wool fiber is a fine, soft, curly hair. It varies in length from four fifths of an inch to four inches. Under a microscope you can see that it is covered with tiny scales overlapping one another like tiles on a roof. The center of the fiber

The way the fibers are shaped makes them good insulators. The waviness of wool fibers keeps the individual fibers from sticking closely together. So cloth made of wool contains many spaces that are filled with air. The still air traps heat. The twisted wool fibers do not cling closely to the body either. A layer of air is formed between the skin and the cloth. This also helps to hold in the body heat.

Wool absorbs moisture from the surrounding air. A pound of wool can contain about two and a half ounces of water, and yet feel perfectly dry. And no machine can squeeze the

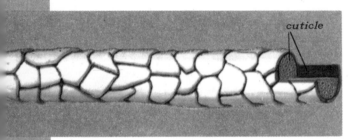

A wool fiber is covered with overlapping scales. This greatly enlarged diagram shows the scales and the inner substance, called the cuticle.

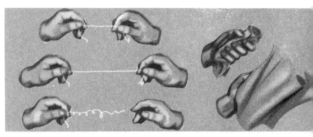

Wool is elastic. If you stretch a fiber, it returns to its original length. Or if you crumple a piece of woolen cloth, it straightens itself out.

is made up of a substance called the cuticle. In the cuticle there is a canal which often contains marrow, a fatty substance.

A wool fiber is elastic and will stretch when it is pulled slowly. After a fiber has been stretched, it returns very slowly to its original length and its wavy shape. Because of this quality, clothes made of wool cloth will smooth themselves out if they are hung up after having been worn, and the wrinkles will disappear.

Wool protects the body from the cold better than any other fabric. The human body is always producing heat. The temperature of the body is about 98.6 degrees Fahrenheit, but usually you feel comfortable—neither hot nor cold —if the temperature of the air is about 70 degrees. The body is continuously giving up heat to the air that surrounds it. The main purpose of clothing is to slow down this loss of body heat. Wool keeps the body warm because it is a poor conductor of heat.

water out. In the same way wool rapidly absorbs perspiration and gives you a feeling of dryness. In the process of absorbing moisture, wool also produces a small amount of heat.

When you leave the house in winter, and go out into the cold, wet air, the wool of your clothes absorbs part of this dampness and produces heat. At the same time it helps to keep the heat of your body from escaping into the air and therefore keeps you warm.

Sheep are usually shorn once a year. This happens in the spring, so that their coats can grow back before winter. The wool fibers are separate, but grouped into a large number of tufts or locks. So the fleece comes off in one piece like a blanket, and after being shorn off, looks almost as it does when it is attached to the sheep.

When the shorn fleeces come to the woolen mill, they are sorted according to which part of the sheep they came from. Each part of the fleece gives a wool of a different quality. Then the wool, which is full of dirt and animal grease, is cleaned in a special machine called a leviathan. The wool is put into an enormous boiler filled with water and detergents. It is stirred around mechanically by huge forks until it is completely clean. The grease from the wool is taken from the water and used to make lanolin, the basis of many ointments.

Then the wool is carded. In ancient times, shepherds pulled masses of thistles across the shorn fleece to make the wool softer, smoother, and cleaner. In later days, housewives worked the wool back and forth between two boards covered with points. Now this work is done by machines. They have large cylinders studded with points that turn against each other. Carding separates the fibers and makes the wool much softer. After carding, the fiber is ready to be spun into yarn.

The wool comes out of the carding machine in the form of a thin sheet which is then separated into strips called slivers. Or the carded wool can be combed by being passed through combs in a machine. This divides the wool into broad slivers made of parallel fibers.

The carded or combed wool is then spun into thread by being stretched and twisted on a machine. Threads differ in thickness according to the number of fibers they are composed of. In some fine wools, as much as 50,000 yards of yarn can be obtained from one pound of wool. This yarn is wound on spools called spindles. The spindles are put into a loom, and the thread is woven into warm cloth.

The woolen textile industry is a very large and important one. In New England it was for many years the most important industry. Australia produces huge amounts of wool for exporting. Argentina, the U.S.S.R., and New Zealand also produce a great deal of wool for clothing and carpets.

In a carding machine, the wool fibers are cleaned, smoothed and softened. The bulk of the fibers becomes much greater.
(1) Carded wool is bulky and soft. (2) Combed wool is divided into slivers made of parallel fibers.

Woolen cloth does not stick to the skin. There is always a layer of air between them. (1) skin (2) woolen cloth (3) fibers that hold the cloth away from the skin (4) air layer which insulates better than wool itself

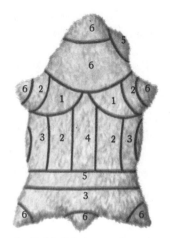

A fleece is divided into sections of different qualities, numbered from one to six according to excellence.

Plant Cells

All living matter is made up of cells. They are so small you cannot see them. Under a microscope a cell would look like a tiny room with walls around its edges. The word cell comes from a Latin word that means little room.

A cell is the smallest form of life. It eats, reproduces by making more cells of its own kind, and grows and dies, as all living things do. Any living thing is called an organism—a man, a rose, the smallest cell that cannot be seen, and the largest tree. There are organisms made of billions of cells, and some of only one cell. The smallest bacteria are one-celled, while elephants are made of billions of cells.

In 1665 an Englishman, Robert Hooke, published the results of his work in examining pieces of cork under a microscope. He was the first to use the word cell to describe what he saw. After the cells in cork had been discovered, scientists wondered whether other parts of a tree besides the cork might have such cells. They found them in roots, leaves, wood, seeds, and flower parts. Similar divisions were also found in animal organisms such as skin and

This is a greatly enlarged diagram of a plant cell.

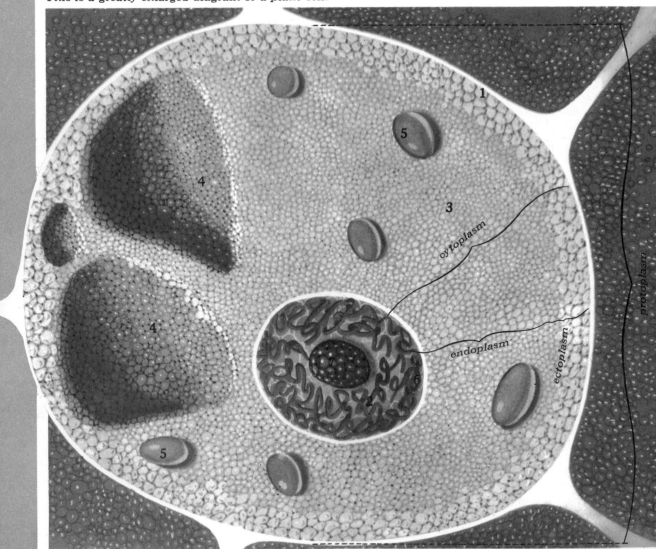

Robert Hooke drew cork cells in about 1665 from his view of them under a microscope.

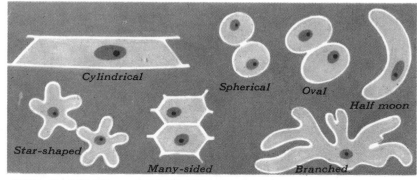

Cylindrical

Spherical

Oval

Half moon

Star-shaped

Many-sided

Branched

THE VARIOUS SHAPES OF VEGETABLE CELLS

nucleus

vacuoles

vacuoles

nucleus

The vacuoles expand as the cells stretch and grow old.

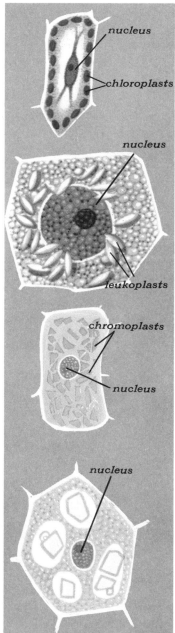

nucleus

chloroplasts

nucleus

leukoplasts

chromoplasts

nucleus

nucleus

Green chloroplasts

White leukoplasts

Colored chromoplasts

THE DIFFERENT PLASTIDS IN THE CYTOPLASM

A magnified view of vacuoles containing grains of substances such as sugar, oils and fats secreted by the cell.

muscle tissue. Finally, by the 19th century, there was enough evidence to prove that all living things are made of cells.

Plants are organisms made up of microscopic cells. The cells come in different shapes and sizes. They are round, square, oval, many-sided, branched—almost any shape that can be imagined.

Every plant cell, even though it can't be seen without a microscope, has different parts. The outside walls of a vegetable cell are called the cellular membrane (1). Inside these walls is a jellylike substance called the protoplasm. The protoplasm is the living stuff of the cell, and the cell membrane is dead. The part of the protoplasm that is near the center of the cell is called the nucleus (2). The rest of the protoplasm between the cell wall and the nucleus is called the cytoplasm (3).

The dead cellular membrane is made from a substance given off by the cytoplasm—threads interwoven into a material called cellulose. The cell membrane protects the cytoplasm and acts as a support by holding it in.

Although the cytoplasm looks like jelly, it is 70 to 80 percent water. The rest of it is made up of about 40 other chemical elements such as carbon, hydrogen, oxygen, nitrogen, phosphorus, potassium, sulphur, calcium, magnesium, and iron.

The cytoplasm also has holes in it called vacuoles (4). These vacuoles are a very important part of the cytoplasm. Inside them are sugars, acids, oils, and fats. It is these substances that make various plants valuable to man. For example, the sugar in grapes, sugar cane, and sugar beets is an important food in the human diet. Citric acid in lemons, oranges, and grapefruits is also valuable. And the oils and fats in seeds, resins, and some herbs are used in industry and in medicine.

The cytoplasm is divided into two parts, the inner area and the outer area nearest the cell wall. The outer part is called the ectoplasm. This part lets water and the mineral substances in it pass through to the center of the cell.

The inner part of the cytoplasm is called the endoplasm. The endoplasm is always in motion. Under a microscope it looks as if it flows in currents, like a river. This movement is caused by chemical changes that are always taking place within the cell.

Also floating in the cytoplasm are small granules called plastids (5). There are different

called photosynthesis. The living cells in a green plant get their food—sugar—by making it. When the sun goes down at night the process stops.

Some of the sugar the plant cells have made is used as food. Some of it is changed into starch and stored in the pith of the plant. The part of the cytoplasm that makes sugar into starch is the leukoplast. Like the chloroplasts, leukoplasts are small, white, round or oval plastids.

Still another plastid is the chromoplast. These plastids change the green color of plants to yellow, orange, or red. This process occurs when a green apple ripens to red and when leaves turn red and yellow in the fall.

The center of the cytoplasm is the nucleus. This is a small structure, shaped like an egg. It has its own wall called a nuclear membrane (6). Inside the nucleus are small grains of material called nucleoles (7) which are proteins. There are also tiny particles—chromosomes— that pass on hereditary characteristics from one generation of a plant to the next. When the

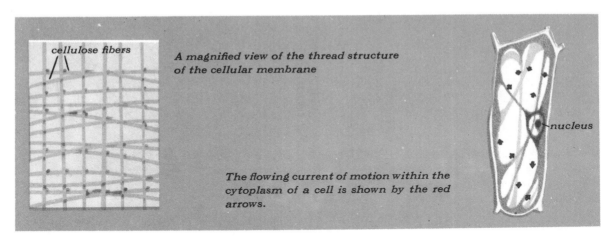

cellulose fibers

A magnified view of the thread structure of the cellular membrane

The flowing current of motion within the cytoplasm of a cell is shown by the red arrows.

nucleus

kinds of plastids—chloroplasts, chromoplasts, and leukoplasts. Each of these has an important job in the life of the cell.

Chloroplasts contain the green coloring matter of plants called chlorophyll. The job of chlorophyll is to cause chemical changes in the plant. Carbon dioxide from the air and water from the roots enter a plant cell. The chloroplasts in the cell unite with the water and the carbon dioxide to form sugar, using the energy of sunlight in the process. This process is

plant reproduces, its nucleus divides, forming two nuclei, and thus characteristics are transmitted to the new cells. Such traits as shape, strength, length of life, and size are contained in this part of the nucleus. This is why the seed of a daisy plant makes another daisy, not some other plant.

It is hard to believe that a single cell, too small to see without a microscope, could be so complicated. Yet all the processes of life take place in this tiny organism.

Sparrows

Sparrows are one of the largest families of birds, the perching birds. The family covers many varieties, from the nightingale to the swallow, from the lyrebird to the lark. And within this large group, the sparrows themselves belong to various categories—buntings, for instance, or finches, grosbeaks or juncos. Sparrow in general is a term used for a number of small birds who have little in common except their size.

The sparrow we know best in the United States and in Europe and Asia is the house sparrow, or English sparrow. It is actually a member of the weaver finch family. It has a gray crown and a black throat, and its wings are marked by a chestnut and white bar which has a black border. It is about six inches long, and its song is a harsh chirp.

The English sparrow does not go to warmer places in the winter, although there are other kinds of sparrows which do. It is at home both in the city and in the country. Even when the ground is covered with snow it can usually find food, since it eats both insects and seeds. In a large city there are generally crumbs to be found on streets and on window sills, and it is a common sight to see sparrows flocking where pigeons are fed in the parks. Being tiny and aggressive, they can dart beneath the pigeons' beaks to take the food away from them.

Instead of walking, sparrows jump with both feet together. A man moving in a similar way would have to jump 10 to 12 feet each time.

Most birds rise from the ground sharply. The sparrow rises slowly as if it did not want to get too far from its source of food.

A sparrow's nest is not a thing of beauty. It is built from any sort of material—grass, twigs, straw, plant stems, hair, moss, or trash—and arranged in any fashion. Sparrows will not hesitate to drive away other birds who have selected the same tree branch or corner of a house to build their own nests. In some cases sparrows

The Italian sparrow lives only in Italy. It has bright white cheek patches, a reddish crown, and a black area at its throat.

have even been known to take over the more carefully constructed nests of other birds by driving the owners away.

Sparrows lay four to six eggs of a grayish-white color, usually spotted with brown. Throughout the warmer months of the year sparrows lay brood after brood. Sometimes if there is an unseasonable warm spell in winter, the male sparrow will begin courting the female again, hopping about with his wings down and his tail spread out, chirping noisily. Both male and female sparrows are attentive parents to the young birds when they are hatched out. They feed their young and guard them until they are able to fly away. After that, like most other birds, sparrows are on their own.

The history of the English sparrow in the United States and Australia is a curious one. The birds were not native to these countries, but were imported from Europe in the middle of the 19th century. The 50 birds which were originally brought to Australia have multiplied by millions. The sparrows that were brought to New York have spread all over the United States and parts of Canada and Mexico.

The sparrows were originally imported because they attacked a certain canker worm which was destroying trees. Unfortunately, the change of climate affected the birds' eating hab-

English sparrows that live in cities are often so dirty they seem to be different birds from country English sparrows.

The European tree sparrow has been imported to the middle western United States. It has a black spot behind the eye.

The sparrow's beak is short and strong. It is built for cracking seeds.

The beaks of insect-eating birds are long and slim. They are adapted to catching insects in flight.

The republican sparrows of Africa live in large groups. Their roofed nests are sometimes as big as a man's hut.

its, and instead of attacking the insect blight, they devoured the seeds from the farmers' fields. In addition to this, the English sparrows attacked such native birds as wrens, martins, bluebirds, and thrushes. Often sparrows have been known to destroy other birds' young.

This unpopular little bird has been called tramp, hoodlum, and other such unfavorable names. In England, the House of Commons formed a special committee to decide whether the sparrow's ability to destroy insects made up for its general destructiveness. And as early as 1895, the Department of Agriculture in Washington prepared a report on the advantages and disadvantages of sparrows. Of the sources they quoted, 168 were in favor of sparrows, 43 were neutral, and 837 were so strongly against them that they recommended the destruction of the eggs and nests. The number of sparrows is decreasing somewhat.

Since the English sparrow lives in both the city and the country, it is a more familiar sight than others of the sparrow family. There are some, however, which have more pleasant characteristics and are better liked.

The song sparrow is a somewhat larger bird. Its clear, gay song can be heard throughout most of the year except in the coldest winter months. It is known as the most constant singer of all North American songbirds.

The vesper sparrow is also a songbird, though its voice is not as loud as the song sparrow's. It sings most frequently in the late afternoon, which is why it is given its name.

The tree sparrow, with its reddish crown, dark brown back, and white-barred brown wings, is also familiar in the United States. It does not migrate in winter. Other sparrows such as the chipping sparrow or the field sparrow fly south during the winter months.

There are native types of sparrows in every part of the world, except in Australia, to which they were imported. The Italian sparrow, for instance, makes its home only in Italy. The Sardinian or Spanish sparrow lives in North Africa, Sardinia, and Sicily. The republican sparrow lives in Africa and gets its name because it builds community houses and lives in them with other sparrows.

Knights in Armor

Knights were originally a king's mounted soldiers. Under the feudal system, the king gave parts of his lands to various persons, who in return agreed to fight for him. They usually fought in his armies for about forty days each year. The great lords received their land directly from the king. They distributed small parts of it to lesser nobles, who were called knights. In wartime, the lord went into battle at the head of his own group of knights.

Each knight supplied his own horses, armor, and weapons. He also had to support one or more squires and pages. Pages were apprentice knights, often the young sons of the

Young men and boys were taught to handle all kinds of weapons.

A young man is being knighted. The words used might have been: "In the name of God, St. Michael, and St. George, I dub thee knight."

knight's friends, and squires were somewhat older servants, young men who had gone further in training for knighthood.

This training was very arduous. The pages and squires had to learn to ride, fight, swim, hunt, and handle all kinds of weapons. They had to be obedient, and their upbringing was very strict. They also received a little formal education, though not too much. Many knights could not read or write.

There were two ways to become a knight. One was very simple. If a young squire or soldier distinguished himself in war, by fighting bravely or risking his life for his lord or king, he might be knighted on the spot. He knelt before his lord, who struck him on the shoulder with his sword, and then told him to rise. From that moment he was a knight.

In peacetime, or in the case of the sons of kings and nobles, the procedure was more complicated. The young man usually had to serve first as a page, then as a squire, until he was twenty-one years old. The day before the ceremony for knighthood, he took a bath to signify that he was purified of sin. He then put on a white tunic as a symbol of this purity. He went without food until the next day. He spent the night in the chapel of the castle with his arms and armor. This was the Knightly Vigil, or Vigil of Arms.

In the morning he was dressed in his armor and blessed by the priests. Then his spurs, the symbol of knighthood, were fixed to his heels. He knelt before the altar, and his lord struck him three times on the shoulder with his sword. According to a sacred formula, which varied in different places, the lord declared him a knight.

Not all knights were soldiers in a king's army. Some were knights errant. These knights traveled about with their squires, going from castle to castle and seeking adventure along the way. All knights were sworn to uphold the code of chivalry. A knight errant was supposed to protect church property, defend the weak, and be liberal and generous to everyone. He was sworn to be a champion of justice against

A knight is intervening in a quarrel between some armed men and a group of defenseless civilians. They are three to his one, but the knight is mounted on a horse, so he is not outclassed.

An exciting and dangerous part of a tournament was a free-for-all, in which teams of knights fought each other.

all evildoers. He was supposed to fight brigands and thieves, and protect widows and orphans.

There are many more knights errant in the romantic stories of chivalry than there were in real life. Most knights were simply soldiers. Life in the Middle Ages was often savage and cruel, so the knights were savage and cruel too. Knights are imagined going about righting wrongs and fighting on the side of the poor and downtrodden, but this happened very seldom. An armed man on a horse had a great advantage over almost everyone he met in his travels. And only a man with great self-control and discipline could resist the temptation to take what he could get. Many knights took advantage of their position.

However, if a knight broke too many of the rules of chivalry, he could be deprived of his knighthood. His arms, and especially his spurs, were taken from him. His sword was broken over his head and thrown down, with his shield, into the dirt. This was a rare occurrence, but it did happen sometimes.

One of the main activities of knights, besides fighting in wars, was engaging in the tournaments. These contests were held from time to time in various parts of England and on the continent.

At first, tournaments were serious matters. Knights who competed in them were often killed or severely wounded. Later the Church and kings who did not want to lose their best soldiers made rules. Then tournaments became relatively safe. But when, in 1559, a king of France died as the result of an accident in a tournament, they fell into disfavor.

The first tournaments were pitched battles between armed men. Later they became pageants. They were colorful entertainments which were viewed by ladies and gentlemen and common people from many miles around. Knights fought for the honor of their ladies, and they often wore, pinned to their armor, some token such as a flower or handkerchief.

The picture on pages 388 and 389 is a view of a tournament. On the left is a row of shields belonging to the knights. The shields were hung on poles, and a knight who wished to challenge another would strike with his lance at the shield of his foe.

Heralds with trumpets proclaimed the order of events and the names of the participants.

In the center, two armed and mounted knights are fighting with swords. They started fighting with lances, but both lances have been broken and neither has managed to unhorse the other. They must continue to fight until one is declared the winner. The judges stand in the box behind the heralds.

In front of the heralds we see a knight engaging in a ring joust. He rides toward a ring suspended from a pole, and tries to catch it on the point of his lance.

In the background an armed knight stands on a wooden bridge. He has challenged any knight to try to cross. A knight who accepts the challenge must be prepared to fight him with sword and dagger.

To the right of that is a knight riding at full speed toward a dummy figure on a post. He

must strike the outstretched hand of the dummy with his lance. If he does, the dummy will swing around on the post. If the knight is not agile and quick, he will be dealt a sharp blow with the lead balls hung from the other arm of the dummy.

The most splendid of all the events in a tournament was the mock battle between two groups of knights. There were usually 13 on a side. They would ride at each other dressed in full armor and fight first with lances, then with swords, axes, and maces. This was the most dangerous event as well as the most exciting, and the knights were often bruised and wounded.

During the early Middle Ages, the most common armor was chain mail, made of iron links attached together. But chain mail was not

a very good protection against arrows, and as archery improved, armorers discovered how to make clever little hinges and folds so that a man could be completely clothed in solid sheets of steel. The hinges allowed him to move his arms, legs, and fingers inside his almost impenetrable covering.

Armor of chain mail was heavy enough, but a suit of steel plate armor sometimes weighed more than a hundred pounds. Only a mounted man could wear it, and knights dressed in the heaviest tournament and ceremonial armor had to be hoisted onto their horses by a system of blocks and tackles.

Armor reached its greatest peak of development around the end of the 16th century. But by that time gunpowder had been invented, and in a short time armor became obsolete. The age of chain mail and steel plate armor did not much outlast the age of chivalry.

The knight holds a jousting lance in his hand. He will ride at another knight similarly dressed and try to unhorse him by striking his shield with his lance. The shield is curved to deflect the blow.

A knight carried many different weapons in battle and in tournaments. The sword and dagger hung from a belt around his waist, and the axe and mace —war club—were attached to his horse's saddle, where he could easily reach them.

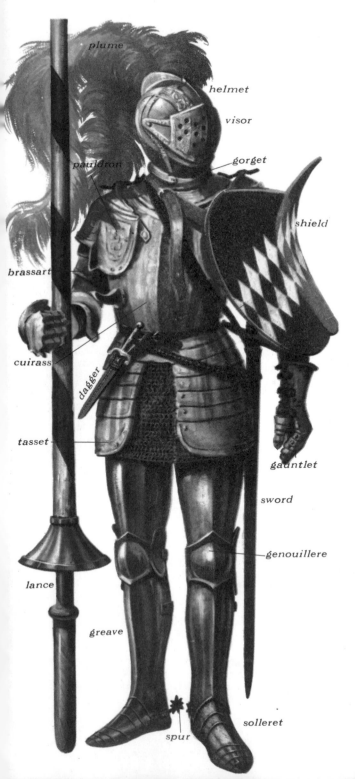

plume
helmet
visor
gorget
pauldron
shield
brassart
cuirass
dagger
tasset
gauntlet
sword
genouillere
lance
greave
spur
solleret

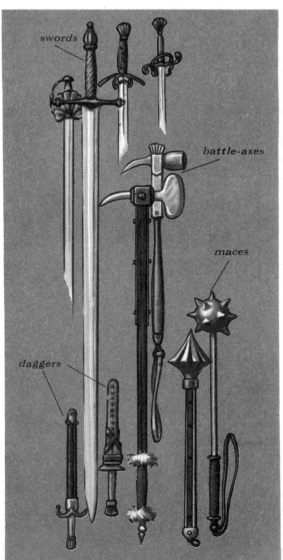

swords
battle-axes
maces
daggers

Light and Color

Human beings have always been curious about the nature of light. The ancient Greeks knew that light traveled in straight lines. By the 18th century men had learned a good deal about reflection and bending of light rays. Yet, even in the atomic age, scientists are still not agreed upon what light really is.

Light is a form of energy, but there is no one scientific theory to explain everything we know about the way that light behaves. Some scientists talk about light traveling in tiny packages of energy called photons. Others think that light travels in the form of waves, like sound waves, but infinitely smaller.

Both explanations can be applied under certain conditions. So the true nature of light is probably a combination of photons and waves. What the combination is, science still has to discover exactly.

Certain properties of light are known. Light is the fastest thing in the universe. It moves more swiftly than anything man can make. It moves in air at about 186,000 miles a second, which is about 11,000,000 miles a minute! This speed was accurately measured by the American physicist A. A. Michelson at the beginning of the 20th century.

But the speed at which light moves depends on the medium through which it is traveling. In space, where there is no air to slow the light down, it moves a little faster than 186,000 miles a second. But in water, glass, and other substances such as gases that are denser than air, light moves more slowly.

REFRACTION OF LIGHT

The difference in the speed at which light travels can be seen when we notice that a drinking straw in a glass of water seems to be bent. Or we may see that the bottom of a swimming pool looks closer than it really is. The straw is not bent and the bottom is not as shallow as it seems. The light that reaches our eyes makes them appear so.

This bending, which takes place when light moves from air to water or water to air, is

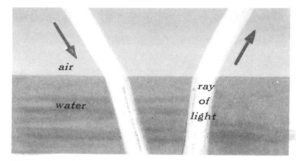

The refraction of light

known as refraction. The bending occurs at the point where the air and water meet. Refraction takes place whenever light moves from a substance of one density to a substance of a different density. The densities of air and glass are different, for example. So are the densities of each liquid and each gas.

Light bends because of the different speeds at which it travels in different substances. Think of a beam of light as a line of soldiers marching across a meadow. The soldiers keep the same speed as long as they are all marching on the grass, which is like the air. But the moment they come to a plowed part of the meadow, they will have to slow down. The earth and mud are harder to march on. The plowed part is more dense than the meadow, as glass is more dense than air.

If the line of soldiers strikes the plowed part at an angle, the line will change direction. The soldiers on the right of the line will be slowed down first, while the soldiers on the left,

An explanation of how light is refracted

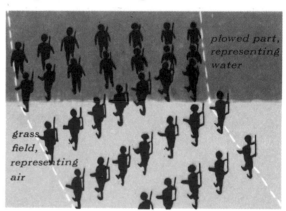

plowed part, representing water

grass field, representing air

who are still on the grass, will keep marching at their original speed. They will tend to turn the line until the time when they reach the plowed part and are slowed down, too. The line of soldiers—or the beam of light—has changed its course. It has been bent.

A straw seems bent when it is partly in water and partly out because we see objects by means of the light that comes from them. If that light is bent by refraction, it seems to come from the wrong place. Then we will see the object in the wrong place. If it is a straw or stick, it will look bent to us.

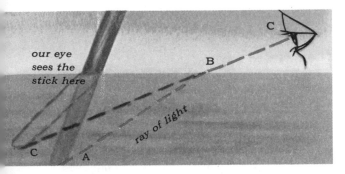

The light ray bends at point B where it leaves the water. As a result, our eye traces the light back to C rather than to A where the end of the stick is.

THE COLORS OF LIGHT

We normally think of light as being white, but there are actually many different colors of light, depending on where the light is coming from. Sir Isaac Newton, the great English scientist, first divided white light into colors. He let a ray of sunlight pass through a crack in the shutters of his darkened room. Then he passed the light through a glass prism onto a screen. The ray of light was split up into a rainbow-colored spectrum in which Newton counted seven main colors: red, orange, yellow, green, blue, indigo, and violet.

If a thermometer is held to the right of the red band of light in a spot where no light can be seen at all, the temperature will go up noticeably. This section of the spectrum is known as infra-red. Infra-red light is not visible to the naked eye. But infra-red is a form of light energy and—like the invisible ultra-violet rays at the other end of the spectrum—is a part of white light that can be separated out by a quartz prism.

The separation of white light into colors is the result of refraction. Imagine that the column of soldiers has been lined up so that the strongest soldier is on one end and the weakest is on the other. As the soldiers enter the plowed part of the field, the weakest one will be slowed down more than the strongest. Then the column of soldiers will become separated. The soldiers—or the colors—will fan out.

Colors can be said to have different strengths because they have different wave lengths. The red light rays, which have the longest wave length and are like the strongest

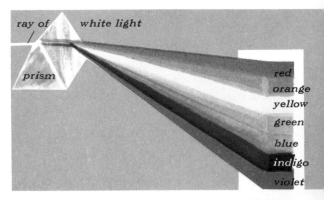

ray of white light
prism

red
orange
yellow
green
blue
indigo
violet

This is what happened when Newton passed white light through a prism.

A ray of white light is separated into seven colors.

long, strong stride
short, weak stride

An explanation of how white light splits into colors

Red, the color with the longest wave length, bends the least. Violet, with the shortest wave length, bends the most.

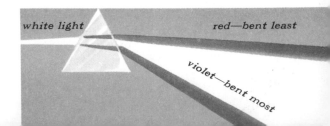

white light
red—bent least
violet—bent most

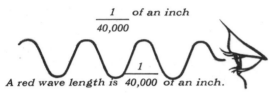

$\frac{1}{40,000}$ of an inch

A red wave length is $\frac{1}{40,000}$ of an inch.

A wave length is the distance between the tops or bottoms of two waves that follow each other.

apple

An apple appears yellow because it reflects only yellow light.

orange

An orange reflects orange, yellow and red, and absorbs all the other colors.

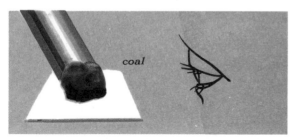

coal

Coal reflects no light, so it appears black.

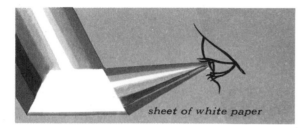

sheet of white paper

The sheet appears white because it reflects all the light that falls on it.

Ordinary glass lets color pass through without change.

glass

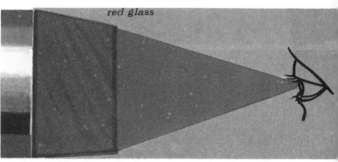

red glass

Light shining through red glass looks red because the red glass filters out all the other colors and lets only red light through.

soldiers, are bent the least. Their wave length is about 1/40,000 of an inch. The violet rays, which have a shorter wave length, are bent more. Their wave length is about 1/66,700 of an inch.

The color we see depends upon the wave length of the light that strikes our eyes. If we see a beam of light with a wave length of 1/40,000 of an inch, we say it is red.

We see that objects are different colors because of the light they reflect back to our eyes. White light contains all colors. If white light falls on a yellow apple, the apple skin absorbs all of the other colors except the color with the wave length of yellow. This light is reflected. It comes back to our eyes, and we see the apple as yellow. An orange skin will absorb all the colors except yellow, orange, and red, which are reflected back.

An object appears to be black when it absorbs all the light and reflects back no light at all. There is no wave length of light that is black. We see black objects because they reflect no light waves, and the colors around them do reflect.

White bodies, on the other hand, seem white because they reflect back all the different wave lengths of light. And all the color wave lengths mixed together make up white light.

Glass, if it is colorless, lets most of the white light pass through unchanged. This is also true of quartz, water, and cellophane. We can see through these objects easily and colors are not changed. But a colored glass such as the red glass in a stop light, filters out or absorbs all the colors except red. As a result, red light is the only light we see.

Europe

Compared with the other continents of the world, Europe is quite small. It has an area of only 4,000,000 square miles. It is about one quarter the size of Asia and one third the size of Africa. But even though Europe is not large, it is very important. Since the continent is small, it is easy to get from one great European city to another. And, except for the Atlantic Ocean, which lies between Europe and the Western Hemisphere, none of the seas which surround Europe is very large. So it is also quite easy to travel from the cities of Europe to the cities on other continents.

For many centuries Europe has been a trading center for people all over the world. They have bought and sold manufactured goods—cameras from Germany, china and lace and perfumes from France, silverware and woolens from England, automobiles from Italy. Delicious cheeses, fruits, and wines also come from European countries.

But Europe is also the center of another kind of exchange. Ever since the beginnings of European history its people have exchanged knowledge about art and books. They have ex-

The continent of Europe is in the middle of the large land masses of the earth, Asia, Africa, and the Americas. From Europe, no other continent is very difficult to reach.

changed ideas about law and religion and philosophy. They have added to the scientific knowledge of the world.

Thousands of years ago the people of Europe did not carry on much trade of any kind because they did not trust each other. To trust other people it is necessary to understand them. But the early Europeans lived in small groups

The ideas, customs, and languages of Europe were spread across the globe by explorers and settlers.

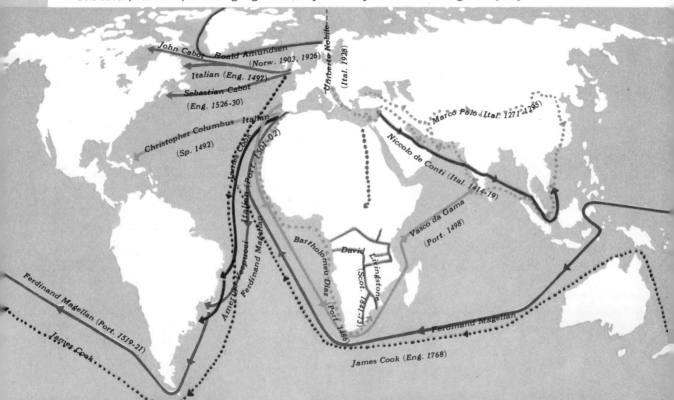

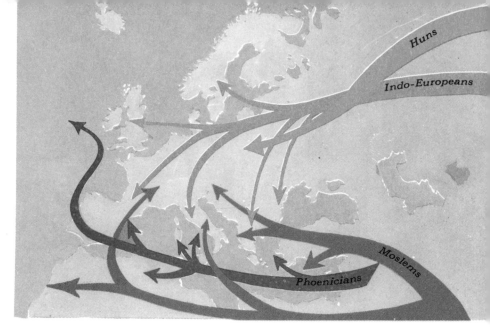

The early European tribes united with one another and then were overrun by peoples from the East. The people of present day Europe are mixtures of all these civilizations.

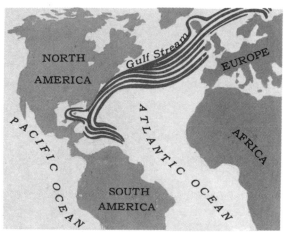

The Gulf Stream, a warm ocean current, passes along the west coast of Europe and is responsible for the mild climate of Great Britain.

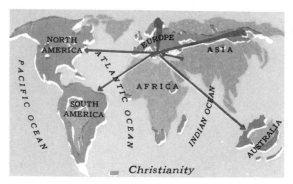

Christianity was born in Palestine. It spread to Europe, and from Europe was carried throughout the world by missionaries and settlers.

called tribes. Each tribe had its own leader and its own laws. Each tribe grew its own food, so no one tribe really needed to visit any other tribe. And since the tribesmen did not visit they could not come to understand and trust the people in other tribes.

The early Europeans belonged to three main groups. The Teutonic groups lived in northern Europe. Most of these people were tall and blond. People of the Mediterranean group lived in southern Europe. They were short and dark. And central Europe was the home of the Alpine group. These people were not especially blond or dark, short or tall.

As the centuries passed and people traveled more, the separate tribes in Europe united. The first thing that brought them together was the civilized ideas of ancient Greece. These ideas were spread to Europe during the fourth and fifth centuries B.C.

Later, during the years between 100 B.C. and A.D. 400, the people of Europe were further unified by the Romans. As the Roman Empire grew larger, the people of Europe were conquered. They all became part of the same civilization. The Roman language, Latin, spread through Europe, and was mixed with the languages already there. From this mixture came our modern Romance languages—French, **Spanish, Italian, Portuguese, and Rumanian**

Early in the fifth century A.D. the weakening Roman Empire was defeated by the barbarian tribes from the east. The barbarians brought more new languages, customs, and laws to Europe. About 400 years later a new system of land ownership developed. It is called the feudal system and it came partly from the customs of the barbarians. Under the feudal system the powers of the state were divided among many lords, who owned large estates.

As time passed, two things happened. The craftsmen of feudal times began to live together in towns. And the lords were given titles. They were called kings, princes, and dukes. And finally, at the end of the 13th century, several European countries became nationalized states. Each state was ruled by a king. The king had all the power and he became the king because some member of his family had been the king before him.

Sometimes a king treated his people badly, and the people became angry and fought against him. Such a war is called a revolution, and there have been many revolutions in Europe. The people who fight in a revolution are usually people who want to be free. This desire for freedom has spread from Europe to many other parts of the world—to North and South America, to China and Indonesia, and to Africa and India.

The idea of freedom is just one of the many ideas the people of Europe have given to the rest of the world. Europeans have been given new ideas too, because many people from other places go to live and visit in Europe. Europe is a good place to live in and an excellent place for a vacation. Europe's climate is usually mild because most of the continent is in the north temperate zone. The mild climate is also caused by the warm winds and waters of the Gulf Stream.

Europe is made up of two huge peninsulas, separated by the Baltic Sea. With the Baltic on the north, the Atlantic on the west, and the Mediterranean on the south, Europe has a long coastline indented by many large and small bays. Along the coast there are lovely fishing villages and beach resorts. Europe's mountains —notably the Caucasus, the Alps, and the Pyrenees—are beautiful to look at and wonderful for skiing and climbing.

Beautiful cities such as Rome, London, and Paris welcome visitors. And everywhere in Europe visitors can enjoy the products of Europe's rich history.

Martin Luther

At the funeral service for the great reformer Martin Luther, he was described by a minister as a man who had never feared anyone. Certainly this man who made such an enormous change in the church of the Middle Ages could never have accomplished what he did if he had been afraid.

Martin Luther was born in Germany in 1483, the son of a man who operated iron smelting furnaces. His family was not wealthy, but they were able to give Luther a good education. He had taken several degrees when, in 1505, he decided to give up worldliness and become a monk. He entered a strict Augustinian monastery, and for the next few years devoted his time to his studies and to teaching at the University of Wittenberg.

In 1510, Luther was sent to Rome on business for his order. What Luther saw in Rome, which was the center of the Catholic Church, disturbed him greatly. He was particularly troubled by what were called indulgences. If a man had sinned, the Church could ask him to do a penance for that sin. If the penance was very harsh, or went on for a long time, the man could give money to the Church and win an indulgence for himself. His sin would be forgiven. This was an old custom, but Luther became concerned because the Church was granting many indulgences and using the money to rebuild St. Peter's in Rome.

Back in Germany again, Luther studied and thought. He was disturbed by the whole idea of penances imposed by the Church. He worked out a theory that he described as "justification by faith." He felt that a man should win his salvation by disciplining himself and by his own faith in God. It was not enough to win forgiveness for sin by a few acts of repentance which the Church told him to perform.

In 1517, Luther wrote 95 theses—arguments against the practice of indulgences. To make sure that many people would read them, he nailed them up on the church door at Wittenberg. The 95 theses created an immediate sensation. Many people were interested, and as Luther continued preaching and writing books on his theory of justification, still others were attracted by his ideas.

In Rome, in 1520, Pope Leo X became convinced that Luther's writings were harmful to the Church. He issued an order giving Luther 60 days to retract the things he had written. If Luther did not do so, he and his followers would be excommunicated. They would be entirely cut off from the Church. The Catholic Church of Luther's time was the only Christian church, and to a deeply religious man like Luther it was a terrible thing to realize that he might no longer take communion, hear mass, or be buried by the Church. But Luther refused to be frightened. At a public gathering, he burned the Pope's order.

In 1521, the Pope excommunicated Luther and asked Charles V, the Holy Roman Emperor, to carry out his order. But by this time Luther had a great many supporters in Germany, including the Elector of Saxony, ruler of the region in which he lived. So the Emperor asked Luther to appear before a parliament, or Diet, of German statesmen in the city of Worms, and to defend his position. Luther appeared at Worms and told the Diet that he would not retract his writings, saying, "I neither can nor will revoke anything, since it is not safe or right to act against conscience."

After this, the Emperor told Luther to leave Worms. But the Elector of Saxony, who feared for Luther's safety, hid him in one of his castles. The Emperor then banned Luther from the whole Holy Roman Empire, though most of the Diet did not agree with this action.

During the year that Luther remained in hiding at the Elector's castle, he translated the New Testament into German. Later he translated the Old Testament as well, and the Luther Bible did much to attract an increasing number of people. They called themselves Protestants because they were protesting against practices they disapproved of.

After a year, Luther returned to Wittenberg, where he went on teaching and writing. The ban against him was never carried out because so many people supported him.

Martin Luther, an Augustinian monk, challenged the Catholic Church and became the leader of a large number of people who called themselves Protestants.

Luther could be said to be the leader of a movement that later was called the Reformation. His teachings appealed to people for many reasons. When he attacked the abuses in the Church he seemed to be urging a kind of democracy that would make all people equal. A German peasant revolution actually took place, inspired by the teachings of Luther and his fellow Protestants.

Luther himself did not approve of the peasant rebellion and urged the German princes to suppress it. But it was his ideas which gave birth to the revolution. He argued, for instance, that priests were no better than other men, and that church services should be in a language understandable to everyone. He did not believe that priests should remain unmarried. He married a woman named Catherine von Bora, who had once been a nun. They had five children and lived happily together for 20 years.

During the last years of his life, Luther revised his translations of the Bible and wrote a number of hymns in addition to his other works. One of them, "A Mighty Fortress Is Our God," is famous. He reformed the Saxon Church so that services were read in German instead of Latin, and he tried to establish general education for children. He died at the age of 63, in 1546. Martin Luther was buried in the same castle church of Wittenberg where he had posted his 95 theses at the beginning of the Reformation.

Egyptian ointment jar, about 1500 B.C.

Bronze mortar for spices, A.D. 1300

17th century jar to hold drugs

Glass retort of the Middle Ages

Pharmacy

Pharmacy means the art of preparing drugs or medicine. Nowadays a pharmacy is a drugstore, and a pharmacist is a man who prepares medicines according to a doctor's prescriptions.

Years ago, the pharmacist and the doctor were the same. The earliest men ate certain herbs because they saw sick animals eat them. These primitive people did not know what caused herbs to work, but they learned to recognize the ones which made them feel better.

Later, medicine became more of a science. In ancient Egypt, doctors prescribed elaborate mixtures of drugs for different diseases. We have pictures of an Egyptian drug factory where plants, parts of animals, and other ingredients were prepared. An Egyptian papyrus scroll has been found which is dated about 1700 B.C. and gives the remedies for many diseases. The Egyptians used minerals as well as herbs. They also used parts of such animals as the mouse, elephant, crocodile, and camel. They used saliva and urine as well as worms and insects to heal patients.

Many of these medicines seem disgusting, but some Egyptian remedies are still used today. They knew how to use opium to kill pain. They prescribed castor oil mixed with beer for stomach ailments. They used yeasts and molds on wounds, although it took thousands of years for us to develop penicillin and antibiotics from the same molds.

The Egyptians embalmed the bodies of their dead as part of their religion. To do this they employed resins, naphtha, and other strongly antiseptic ingredients. The Egyptians were so famous for this medical knowledge that during the Middle Ages and later, the ignorant and superstitious in Europe bought something called mummy powder, which was supposed to protect them from diseases.

The Greeks copied the Egyptians for many of their medicines, but they went further in medical theory. One Greek, Empedocles, divided the body into four elements, or humors as they were called. These elements were hot, cold, moist, and dry. Blood, for instance, was

A deer instinctively eats an herb called dittany to soothe intestinal irritation.

hot. A fever was thought to mean there was too much blood in the body, and it had to be treated with its opposite element, something cool. He recommended cucumber seeds for cooling the body.

Another great Greek who added to our knowledge of drugs was the philosopher Aristotle. He had been the teacher of Alexander the Great, and when the young king conquered Asia and parts of India, he sent specimens of rare plants and animals back to Aristotle. Aristotle wrote an *Inquiry into Plants* which gives much information on medicinal herbs.

In 215 B.C. another Greek doctor described an antidote for snakebite that he called ther-

A bear eats an arum plant to rid itself of worms.

iaca. Theriaca became known as a general antidote for everything, and it was made up of all sorts of ingredients. Sometimes as many as 70 drugs were pulverized and mixed with honey. Theriaca was used until the 18th century.

In ancient Rome there were scholars and doctors who studied plants and animals in order to discover new drugs. But other doctors and pharmacies sold absurd and expensive mixtures of medicine, made out of such things as

This old prescription book contains the formula for the preparation of theriaca. The long list of ingredients was supposed to cure anything from snakebite to tuberculosis.

the blood of turtles and the dung of crocodiles, to cure all kinds of illnesses. One of the greatest of Roman doctors, Galen, tried to expose these false cures.

When the Roman Empire collapsed, much Roman knowledge of medicine disappeared for a time. Healing was in the hands of Christian monks and their monasteries, and for a while it was thought that Greek and Roman remedies were anti-Christian. Fortunately the monks preserved the writings of the great Greek physician Hippocrates and the Roman Galen, and eventually they realized that these writings were worth studying. The monks raised herbs in their gardens and cared for the sick either as visiting doctors or in their own monastery hospitals.

While Europe was in the middle of the Dark Ages, the Arabs were learning a great deal about the science of medicine from Greek literature. Between about A.D. 850 and 1050, the Arabs added to this basic knowledge. They developed chemistry and found many new drugs. They opened the first pharmacies, and used such drugs as camphor, senna, alcohol, borax, and arsenic. They discovered that if they wrapped pills in sweet candy, their patients were more likely to take them. They mixed them with syrups and with rose water and scented their ointments so that they would have

This pharmacist's jar was used for the preparation of theriaca. The jar had to be large or it could not hold all the ingredients.

Ancient Phoenicians used this medicine jar.

A ninth century herbal, a book which described medicinal plants and their properties

doctors of medieval Europe, believed in Empedocles' theory of the four humors. They treated a feverish patient with cold foods. When a patient had a head cold, it meant he had too much phlegm, and he was given hot foods. Another way of getting rid of these humors was by letting out some of the patient's blood. The

A medieval pharmacy

a pleasant odor. Pharmacists had to be licensed and they were forbidden to sell poisons or drugs which might be harmful. Two great Persian doctors, Rhazes and Avicenna, studied the use of drugs, and Avicenna wrote a textbook on medicine which was used for hundreds of years both in Asia and in Europe.

The Arabs and their fellow Asians founded the first medical university in Europe, the University of Salerno, in about A.D. 900. The teachers of Salerno and their pupils, who became the

The cover of a prescription book of 1567

RICETTA
RIO
FIOREN
TINO

The grave monument of a Roman doctor shows a chest which holds his instruments and drugs.

blood was drawn from a vein, or a blood-sucking insect, the leech, was used.

In the 16th century a great doctor, Paracelsus, used chemistry to extract important drugs from minerals and other products of the earth. He did much to get rid of some of the complicated and sometimes useless mixtures of drugs that had been sold in pharmacies up

On this frontispiece of a 16th century German book on pharmacy the doctor is pointing out the ingredients he wants mixed in his prescription.

until then. Explorers of the 15th and 16th centuries traveled to the Far East and to the Americas and brought back other new drugs, such as cinnamon bark from India and balsam from Peru. Tobacco from North America was used to kill pain and to help asthma patients. A little later, in the 17th century, Europeans discov-

ered cinchona bark in Peru. It was called the fever bark by the Indians and could cure malarial fevers and agues, something doctors had tried to do for ages by letting blood or by treating the fever as an overbalance of the heat humor.

In the 18th century, an English doctor named Heberdon exposed some of the old-fashioned remedies such as theriaca. He also made fun of such medicines as mummy powder and toad stones. He convinced London doctors to eliminate many useless drugs from their pharmacopoeia, or listing of drugs.

By the end of the 19th century, more and more new drugs were used. Vaccination for smallpox had been discovered. Anesthetics were being used to ease the pain of patients during operations. Doctors had learned about disinfectants and antiseptics. Pasteur had discovered how to purify milk. The X ray had been developed.

With the 20th century, a whole series of new drugs have appeared in drugstores. Antibiotics, anti-histamines, and tranquilizers are sold. The pharmacist is carefully regulated as to what he can sell and how. Special laws insist that manufacturers may not make false claims about the curing power of their products. There are special standards to measure the ingredients in the doctor's prescription. The modern drugstore is a far cry from the old pharmacy with its stuffed crocodile's skin hanging from the ceiling and its sale of love potions, poisons, theriaca, and mummy powder.

The pharmacy in the monastery of Monte Cassino during the Middle Ages

Joan of Arc told the French Dauphin that she would have him crowned king.

Joan of Arc

In 1429, an army of English soldiers was besieging the French city of Orleans. They had already captured some of the most important cities of France—Paris, Reims, Rouen, and others. The two countries had been fighting over territorial claims for many years. The French king was dead, and his son, the Dauphin Charles, was in hiding at Chinon. He had not been crowned king, and it seemed possible that he never would be. Nowhere in France was there enough strength to resist the English.

It was at this time that the leaders of the English force at Orleans received a letter which said in part: "You, archers, companions of war, gentlemen and others who are before the city of Orleans, go back to your own country . . . you will not hold the realm of France from God; but King Charles, the true heir will hold it; for God wills it. . . . If you do not believe this word, wherever we find you, we shall strike you."

The English leaders were highly amused at this letter, for it was signed with the name of a 17-year-old French peasant girl, Joan of Arc. She had been brought up in her native province of Domremy to tend the sheep, care for her brothers and sisters, and pray in the village church. She could neither read nor write, and she had never in the days of her girlhood handled a weapon. And this was the new champion of France who had promised to lift the siege of Orleans, and have the Dauphin crowned.

Joan of Arc's childhood, until she was 13, was no different from that of the other young people in her village. But at 13, in her father's garden, she believed she heard a voice which she felt came from Saint Michael. Later, other voices spoke to her which she said were those of Saint Catherine and Saint Margaret. At first, these voices told her only to be good and to go to church. But as Joan grew older and became troubled by the war-torn state of her country, the voices told her that she must save France.

When Joan was 16, she went to visit the French squire Robert DeBaudricourt, who commanded the town of Vaucouleurs, a short distance away. She told DeBaudricourt of her mission and she asked him to take her to the Dauphin. At first DeBaudricourt refused to take the 16-year-old girl seriously, and he sent her home. But as she continued to insist that she could save France, he became more impressed by her.

Finally he gave her a horse and a page's suit, and she set out, accompanied by some of De Baudricourt's men. She reached Chinon safely after a long ride through enemy country,

Joan of Arc was born in this house in Domremy.

and sent a letter to the Dauphin asking him to see her. When she was admitted to the court, the Dauphin was standing among his courtiers. No one pointed him out to Joan.

However, she knew him immediately, and she knelt in front of him, saying, "Gentle Dauphin, I am called Joan the Maid, and the King of Heaven tells you by me that you will be crowned in the city of Reims."

The Dauphin was overwhelmed. This young girl who spoke with such authority seemed to him to come as a sign that he would indeed be king. He had her questioned by some of the scholars and churchmen of the country. They all found her to be sincere and truly inspired. So Joan was given armor and troops to lead, and she set off to raise the English siege.

The English were encamped across the Loire River from the French city, where they had been for many months. Joan and her forces crossed the river further upstream when a favorable sailing wind sprang up. They rode into the city, and Joan directed the attack on the English besiegers.

Joan was not a trained soldier, but she instinctively knew when and how to attack. Clad in light armor, she led her men forward and assaulted the British forts. She was wounded once by an arrow, but after resting a bit she returned to the battle. She never gave up. In three days of bitter fighting, Joan helped her men to set the guns, placed scaling ladders against the walls of the English forts, and climbed one herself. The English were driven out of their forts and killed by the hundreds. Joan wept as she

The castle of Chinon where Joan met the Dauphin

saw the number of dead, and she let the last 3,000 English soldiers set out in retreat.

After the relief of Orleans, Joan went on to retake Troyes and Reims. At Reims, her wish was fulfilled, and she saw the Dauphin Charles crowned King of France.

After Reims, Joan marched on to Paris. But her attack on the city failed, and she was wounded again. Later, at Compiegne, Joan was captured in the fighting by a Burgundian archer. She was turned over as a prisoner to the Count of Luxembourg. She was sold by him to the English, who were anxious to take their revenge on this amazing girl who had done them so much harm.

In the city of Rouen, the English gathered a group of French clergymen and scholars from the University of Paris. They were to try Joan as a witch and an unbeliever. There are records of this trial. They show that an uneducated girl, with her direct answers and her firm beliefs, was able to win many arguments against judges who were already set against her. But in the end, their verdict was that she was guilty of the charges. She was sentenced to be burned at the stake as a witch.

On May 30, 1431, Joan was tied to a stake above a great pile of wood in the market square

Joan led the French army at the siege of Orleans.

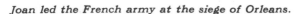

Joan was burned at the stake in the market square of Rouen as a witch and an unbeliever.

Horses

There have been horses on earth for millions of years. There were horses of some kind on earth long before there were men. Something about the first members of the horse family has been discovered from fossil remains.

Prehistoric horses did not look like the horses of today. One of the earliest horses was called the eohippus. The eohippus was only about the size of a fox. Instead of hoofs, it had paws with toes. The eohippus lived in the United States near the Mississippi River at the time when this continent and the continent of Asia were connected. But none of their descendants existed on this continent when Columbus arrived in the western hemisphere.

Many of the little horses wandered from North America to central Asia. During the thousands of years which followed, they became larger and stronger. Some of the wild horses went even farther southwest to the shores of the Mediterranean Sea. The modern horse is descended from the Mediterranean or Arabian horse.

No one knows when horses were first tamed. Prehistoric men used to hunt wild horses and eat them. But many years ago, someone must have realized that horses could be helpful. So men began to capture and tame wild horses. There are almost no naturally wild horses left on earth. But even a tame horse will become very much like its primitive ancestors if it is allowed to run wild. Ponies are good examples of how horses may change. Ponies such

at Rouen. When she asked for a cross, one of the English soldiers handed her one, made of two sticks tied together. As the fire was lighted, she said: "Oh Rouen, Rouen, you shall have great sorrow for my death!"

Twenty-five years later, after the English had been driven out of Rouen, the King of France ordered a retrial of the dead girl. This time, after the questioning of witnesses of the earlier trial, people who had known Joan as a girl, and soldiers who fought with her, Joan of Arc was found to be innocent of the charges.

In 1920, she was canonized as a Saint by Pope Benedict XV.

The horse has a very long head and straight ears.

105

as the Shetland were once the size of regular horses. But they were allowed to run wild. They were affected by the hard climate and poor food, so they became smaller and shaggier and returned to their earlier shape.

The average horse lives to the age of 30 or 40 years. But some horses live to be 50 years old. When horses are just born, they are called foals. Young male horses are called colts and young females are called fillies. When they are full grown, males are called stallions and females are called mares. Horses, especially thoroughbreds, get sick easily. They will get sick if their food is changed suddenly, or if they are given poor food or water. Horses usually eat grass, hay, and various grains.

The horse is an intelligent animal with very well developed senses. A horse can find water in the desert. He can tell his friends from his enemies. He can find the way home even when his master cannot. Horses have excellent memories and very fixed habits. It is difficult to untrain a horse. They are not naturally vicious, but horses will attack men if they have been treated badly, or if a wild mare is protecting her foal and fears for its safety.

There are many different kinds of horses. They are of different shapes, colors and sizes. Most horses are from 14 to 17 hands tall at the shoulder. A hand equals four inches. So a horse that is 15 hands tall is really 60 inches or five feet tall. It takes a heavy, powerful horse to pull heavy loads. Race horses are fast, but far lighter than draught horses.

Most horses have long, coarse hair in their manes and tails. But the rest of their bodies is covered with short soft hair. Their heads are long. The horse's long adaptation to eating hard grasses has resulted in great length of jaw, but little head above the eyes.

Horses' mouths are very sensitive. There is a space between the front and back teeth in a horse's mouth. A bit is placed in the mouth through the space when the horse is ridden. The bit is attached to the reins, and when the reins are pulled or moved from side to side, the bit moves too and presses against the lips. In this way the rider is able to guide the horse and make him go faster or slower.

The different ways a horse travels are called gaits. The average horse uses just four gaits. The slowest gait is a walk. A slightly faster gait is called a trot. The next is a canter, and the smoothest and fastest gait is a gallop. Some horses can gallop at a speed of 40 miles an hour. Usually they go more slowly.

The horse really walks on his toes. The horse's hoof is a toe covered with a hard nail. But the underside of the toe is not hard. Therefore, the underneath part is usually protected by an iron horseshoe. The idea of protecting the

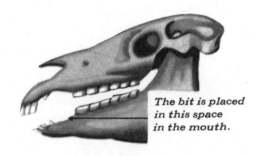

The bit is placed in this space in the mouth.

Members of the horse family put their weight on the single toe at the end of each of their legs.

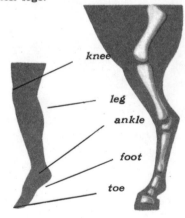

knee

leg

ankle

foot

toe

The toe covering is a hard nail called a hoof.

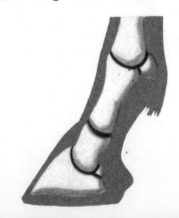

horse's hoof is a very old one. It is so important to protect the hoofs that people have made up a saying about horseshoes, "No shoe, no horse." If a horse's hoof is hurt he cannot walk. And if a horse cannot walk he is no longer useful.

Horses are useful animals. And so are the other members of the horse family. Four other members are the donkey, the mule, the hinny, and the zebra. The donkey, mule, and hinny are closely related. The mule is the offspring of a male donkey and a female horse. The hinny is the offspring of a male horse and a female donkey. Mules and hinnies have no offspring.

All three animals are smaller than horses. They have larger heads and longer ears. They have short manes. All of them are sure-footed and strong. They do not become tired easily. And they are good mountain climbers because they will not slip on rocks even when they are carrying heavy loads. But the donkey and its relatives are also very stubborn animals. So it is not always easy to make them do what you want them to do.

The zebra is a wild horse that looks like a pony. Zebras are creamy white with black stripes. They also have short, stand-up manes. Zebras live in Africa in herds on the grassy plains where there are few trees. The lack of trees and the zebras' sharp eyesight permit them to spot danger even when it is still far away across the plains.

Every different kind of horse and each member of the horse family has developed in its own way. And each, in its own special way, is important to man.

Donkey

Horse

Zebra

Mule

407

Mexicali

San Felipe

Nogales

Cananea

Ciudad Juarez

Río Grande

BAJA CALIFORNIA

SIERRA MADRE

Hermosillo

Sonora

Guaymas

Moctezuma

Ojinaga

Chihuahua

Gulf of California

SIERRA MADRE OCCIDENTAL

6

BOLSON DE MAPIMI

Nueva Rosita

Alamos

Conchos

Rio del Fuerte

4

Nuevo Laredo

SIERRA MADRE ORIENTAL

Mocorito

Reynosa

Gomez Palacio

Torreon

Monterrey

Matamoros

Culiacan

Saltillo

La Paz

1

Santiago

5

Durango

Ciudad Victoria

These two great volcanoes can be seen from Mexico City. They are Popocatepetl in front, and Ixtaccihautl behind it.

Mazatlan

Matehuala

Mezquital

Zacatecas

Panuco

Tampico

Gul

Tepic

Santiago

Aguascalientes

Leon

Guanajuato

Tuxpan

PACIFIC

Guadalajara

Queretaro

Pachuca

2

Tonatlan

Morelia

Mexico City

Jalapa

18,696

Colima

Toluca

Tlaxcala

19,700 FT

Cuernavaca

Puebla

Orizaba

Cordo

Balsas

IXTACCIHUAL 17,342 FT

La Union

Chilpancingo

Acapulco

Oaxaca

Verde

Ometepec

OCE

8,000		Toluca	Zacatecas	
6,600	Mexico City		Puebla	
5,400				
4,200				
3,000				

Many of Mexico's cities are at a great altitude.

Scale of Miles

0   50   100   200   300

Mexico

The Republic of Mexico covers an area larger than Germany, Great Britain, and France together. It runs 1,900 miles from its northernmost and southernmost points, and connects North America to Central America.

Two fingers of land, or peninsulas, extend from Mexico. One, on the northwest coast, reaches into the Pacific Ocean and is called Baja California. The other, on the southeastern coast in the Gulf of Mexico, is Yucatan.

Following Mexico's long coast lines at some distance inland are two mountain ranges known as the Sierra Madres. The western Sierra Madre is a continuation of the North American Rocky Mountains. The eastern range is volcanic mountain. Many of its great peaks are no longer active, but some, like Popocatepetl, still erupt occasionally. The highest of these volcanic mountains are Mount Orizaba and Mount Citlaltepetl at the southern end of the range.

Between the mountain ranges, in the center of Mexico, is a great tableland built up by centuries of volcanic activity and lava. Mexico City, the capital of Mexico, is built on this broad stretch of tableland, which is very high, ranging from 3,500 to 8,000 feet.

There is a great variety of country in Mexico. Part of it is desert, part is tropical jungle. There are high mountain peaks and beautiful beaches. The climate changes from tropical to the cool air of Mexico City, which averages 63 degrees Fahrenheit all year round.

Mexico's rich soil yields a variety of important minerals. Silver, gold, copper, lead, and zinc are some of its many important products. Mexico also has an enormous oil industry and supplies natural gas to the United States. Farming and cattle raising are also important industries. Mexico's products include coffee, corn, citrus fruits, tomatoes, tobacco, cocoa, potatoes, sugar cane, and 50 percent of the world's supply of sisal, a cactus fiber which is used in making rope.

The people of Mexico represent a great mixture of races. The original Mexicans were Indi-

This map of Mexico shows the great variety of country: (1) plateau, covered by material from volcanoes, (2) high tableland, (3) 25 volcanoes, some still active, (4) Western Sierra Madre range, (5) Eastern Sierra Madres, (6) Great Desert, (7) Baja California, (8) Yucatan, the land of the Mayas.

MEXICO
AREA: *760,373 square miles*
POP: *32,350,000*
CAPITAL: *Mexico City*
RELIGION: *Roman Catholic*
LANGUAGES: *Spanish, Indian*
MONETARY UNIT: *Peso (8¢)*

Helmet and sword worn by the Spanish conquistadores who first occupied Mexico

ideas were sweeping Europe. This time, the mestizos, led by a priest, Father Miguel Hidalgo y Costilla, revolted. They captured the northern mining town of Guanajuato and threatened to take Mexico City. In 1811, however, they were defeated, and Hidalgo was executed. After this another priest, Morelos, continued the battle and actually drafted a republican constitution. He was defeated, however, in 1815 and was also executed.

Ironically enough, Mexico's independence was won not by the Indians and their leaders but by wealthy Spaniards who were afraid of

Tepotzotlan Cathedral. The Spaniards converted the Indians to Christianity and built churches in the Spanish style.

ans, but even here there was a great difference between the tribes. When the Spanish conquered Mexico the first colonists to settle the country were men. As a result, there was much intermarrying. Negro slaves were imported by the Spanish to do some of the work, and they too intermarried with the Indians. The descendants of the Spanish and Indians are called mestizos. The pure-bred Spanish are called Creoles.

When Hernando Cortes, the Spanish conquistador, first landed in Mexico in 1519, he and his men conquered the Aztecs, who ruled Mexico City and the surrounding countryside under their king, Montezuma. Under Cortes, the land was proclaimed New Spain and it was ruled by a system called *encomiendas*. The Spaniards were supposed to protect all the Indians on their land, and the Indians in return were to work for the Spanish landlords. Actually the Indians were almost slaves. In 1542, the church protested against the *encomiendas* but the law was not abolished until the 18th century.

Mexico's independence came about shortly after the French Revolution, when republican

the new, more liberal laws in Spain. In 1821, a Spanish army officer named Iturbide forced the last Spanish viceroy to sign a treaty of Mexican independence, making Mexico a separate country.

Miguel Hidalgo y Costilla led Mexico's first revolution.

After proclaiming the independence of Mexico, General Iturbide, a Spanish army officer, had himself crowned emperor.

General Santa Anna gave Mexico a new federal constitution.

Mexico in 1819
Mexico today

Iturbide set himself up as an emperor of Mexico, but his reign did not last long. Another army officer, Santa Anna, led a rebellion against him and installed a federal government of Mexico with its first president, Felix Fernandez, called Guadalupe Victoria.

At this time, what is now the state of Texas belonged to Mexico. Texas had been colonized mostly by men from the United States. They wished to withdraw from Mexico and become part of the United States. Santa Anna led troops to Texas to combat this threat, but he was defeated by Sam Houston at San Jacinto. Later, American troops led by General Winfield Scott came into Mexico and took Mexico City. There a treaty was signed, ceding Texas as far south as the Rio Grande River to the United States.

In 1858, one of Mexico's greatest heroes, the full-blooded Zapotec Indian Benito Juarez, became president. Educated as a lawyer, Juarez drew up a new constitution for Mexico which established greater equality for the people and less power for the church and army. Juarez was the first to gain recognition from foreign countries, such as the United States, Great Britain, and France. He obtained loans of money from these countries to help put Mexico on its feet. But there were many political crises in Mexico, and when Juarez had to ask for a postponement of payment on the loans, Great Britain, France, and Spain decided to intervene in Mexico. French troops attacked in large forces and succeeded in taking Mexico City, driving the Juarez government into exile. The conservatives in Mexico were delighted, and at the suggestion of Napoleon III offered the rule of Mexico to Maximilian of Austria.

Maximilian accepted and was crowned emperor of Mexico. But the conservatives were disappointed in him since he refused to change many of Juarez' reforms, and he lost their backing. At this time the United States was deep in its own Civil War. But in 1865, after the Union victory, the United States government ordered the French to withdraw their armies from the American continent. Napoleon agreed, and in 1866 the last of the French troops were withdrawn, leaving Maximilian with little military support. Maximilian's wife, the Empress Carlotta, went to France to plead with Napoleon to save her husband. Her mission was unsuccessful, and she went hopelessly insane as a result. Maximilian himself was easily conquered by the forces of Juarez and Porfirio Diaz, a mestizo who had long opposed Juárez but supported him in the fight against Maximilian. Maximilian was executed in 1867.

After Maximilian's death, Juarez resumed the presidency and was re-elected in 1871, but died a year later. Diaz seized control of the government and made himself dictator. Except for one short period, he ruled Mexico for 34 years, until 1911.

Diaz did much to build up the economy of Mexico. He built railroads and factories and gave employment to many Mexicans. On the other hand, Diaz retained power only by ruthlessly putting down any uprising of the people. He also divided Mexican land in such a way that it was owned by a very few men, and three fifths of the population were almost serfs.

In 1911 a rebellion gave the presidency to a liberal, Madero. Madero was succeeded by Carranza, and under him, in 1917, Mexico adopted a new constitution which broke up the large landholdings and redistributed the land among the small Mexican farmers. This constitution, which still exists today, provides for a president with a six year term of office who may not be re-elected. In 1958 Adolfo Lopez Mateos became the president of Mexico.

Octopus, Cuttlefish, and Squid

Octopuses, cuttlefish, and squids belong to the class of marine animals known as cephalopods. This name is made up of two Greek words meaning head and leg. Cephalopods have large heads with a number of tentacles, or legs, arranged around the mouth.

There are two main kinds of cephalopods, those that have eight tentacles and those that have 10. The first kind are called octopods, and the commonest variety is the ordinary octopus. The second kind are called decapods, and they include cuttlefish and squids.

There are several other kinds of cephalopods. The most famous is the primitive variety called the chambered nautilus. It has about 90 tentacles, and it lives in a shell which it makes larger every year.

Squids are long, their bodies shaped like a flattened cylinder pointed at one end. At the other end are the mouth and the 10 tentacles which surround it. The fins are triangular. Most squids are small. But the giant squid, which lives in mid-ocean and is sometimes found on Nantucket beaches, can grow to a length of 50 feet. It is the largest animal with no backbone. Those people who report that they have seen a sea monster serpent probably have only seen a giant squid.

A cuttlefish looks as though it is enclosed in a bag, with only its head and legs sticking out. This bag is called a mantle. Inside it are

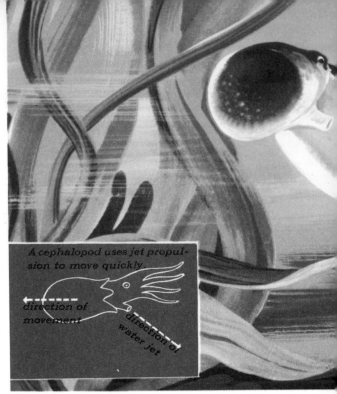

A cephalopod uses jet propulsion to move quickly. direction of movement — direction of water jet

the organs of digestion and reproduction, and the circulatory and respiratory systems. Surrounding the mantle is a pair of fins. The cuttlefish moves them slowly in the water and thus moves itself from place to place.

An octopus has no fins. Instead, it walks on its eight legs, moving slowly along the sea bottom looking for food.

When a cephalopod wants to move quickly, it shoots out a stream of water. The water is stored inside the mantle, and ejected from an organ called a funnel near its mouth. This acts like jet propulsion. The animal moves in the direction opposite to the water jet, and thus escapes backwards from danger. If an enemy such as a large fish or a man approaches, the cephalopod can eject a dark brown substance with its water jet. Then the surrounding water turns dark and hides the fleeing animal from its pursuer. This substance is called ink. The coloring matter known as sepia is made from it.

The octopus is probably the best known of the cephalopods, because of the stories about its fearsome behavior. The stories are usually exaggerated, but there is some truth in them. A large octopus hiding in a sea cavern is a very unpleasant creature to meet. Its mouth is especially hideous. It is hidden in the center of the

The chambered nautilus has 90 tentacles.

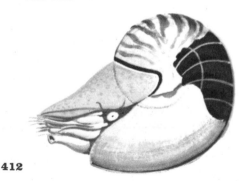

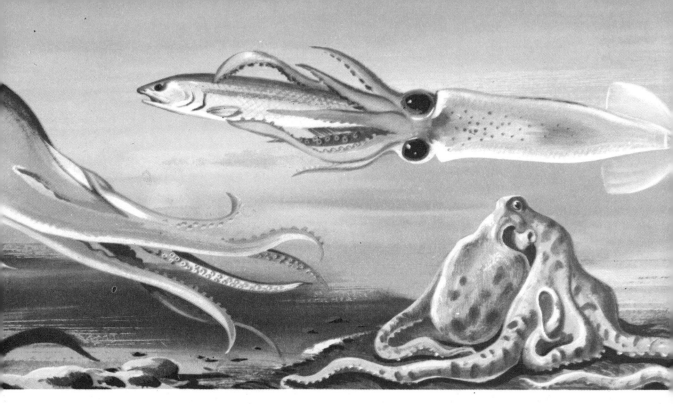

(*At left*) *An octopus walks lazily along the ocean floor. Octopuses can change color. (At right) An octopus has taken on the green color of the rock on which it is resting. (At center) A squid is eating a herring. The two long tentacles hold the prey, and the others move it into the large mouth.*

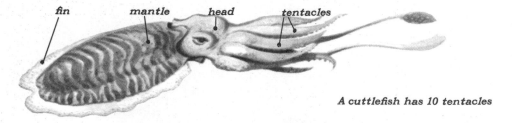

fin   mantle   head   tentacles

A cuttlefish has 10 tentacles

By peeling back the mantle of a cuttlefish, we can see how the animal is constructed. It has three hearts. Two of them are placed at the junction of the gills and the body and serve to pump used blood to the gills from the body. In the gills, the blood absorbs oxygen and then is pumped to the central heart which sends it to the rest of the body.

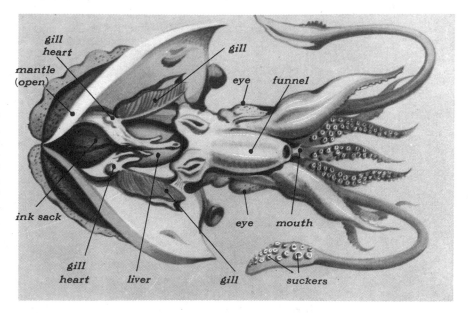

gill heart   gill

mantle (open)   eye   funnel

ink sack

gill heart   liver   gill   eye   mouth   suckers

waving tentacles, but a fish about to be eaten can see it plainly. It consists of two horny projections like a parrot's beak, and inside it is a tongue-like organ called a radula. The radula is covered with sharp teeth, and as the tentacles pull the prey into the mouth, the teeth scrape it and grind it so that it will be more easily digested.

If a diver carrying a knife encounters a large octopus in the water, he should not try to cut off the tentacles which the octopus winds around him. They are covered with suction cups and have very few nerves, so the octopus will not feel the wounds. In captivity, octopuses will sometimes even eat their own tentacles. Instead, the diver should try to stick his knife midway between the octopus' eyes. If he is successful, the knife will strike the brain and kill the animal immediately.

Most octopuses are small and, like small squids and cuttlefish, they are considered a delicacy in certain parts of the world. Italians and Spaniards fry little octopuses and eat them as appetizers, or cut up the legs of larger ones and pickle them or marinate them in oil. Large squids are the basic food of sperm whales. Squids are harvested by the ton from the sea, cut up and used as bait for other fish, and dried and ground up for fertilizer.

Cuttlefish and squids are very much alike, but cuttlefish have a bone inside their bodies, called the cuttlebone, which squids do not have. Ground up, this bone makes a good toothpowder, and centuries ago Roman ladies used it for a cosmetic.

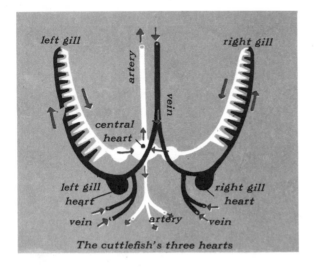

The cuttlefish's three hearts

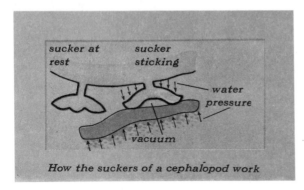

How the suckers of a cephalopod work

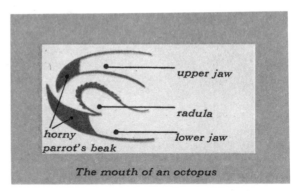

The mouth of an octopus

A cephalopod can throw out an inky substance to color the water so it can hide from the enemy.

Ancient Stone Monuments

Scientists learn about the past by reading documents that were written hundreds of years ago or by finding objects that were made by ancient people, such as tombs, bowls, parts of houses, and so on. Sometimes all they find is a gigantic monument of stones, without any other trace of the people who built them. They call these monuments megaliths because *mega* means giant and *lith* means stone in Greek.

Two examples of the works of megalithic peoples still exist at Carnac in France and at Stonehenge in England. Although many men

this giant circle there was a second circle made up of 40 smaller stone pillars. The stones in this second circle are called foreign stones by specialists, because the kind of rock from which they were made is not found anywhere else within 180 miles!

No one knows exactly how to explain the building of the monuments, or how the giant rocks were carried 180 miles or more. One idea is that the people who built the megaliths originally lived where the foreign stones are found. They built a temple there to worship their gods.

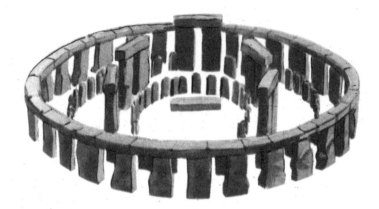

This is what the monument at Stonehenge looked like when it was first built. Only about half the stones are still standing today.

have looked carefully, no other signs have been found of the everyday lives of the people who lived in these places thousands of years ago.

The stones that are still standing at Stonehenge show that originally the monument was made up of 30 giant stone pillars which supported a raised circle of huge stones. The largest of the pillars is nearly 30 feet high. Inside

One day they had to move, perhaps to find more food. Since they didn't want to leave the religious temple behind, they moved it stone by stone to their new settlement. But this theory still doesn't explain how primitive men could move such heavy stones, or how they could lift up the giant stones that rest on the top.

The stones at Carnac are much simpler in

The stones at Carnac were probably put up 2,000 years before the birth of Christ.

There were five huge trilites at Stonehenge. Trilite means three stones. The supporting pillars are more than 25 feet high.

design. But they are still very large stones, and it is a great mystery just what they are doing there and who put them up.

At Carnac the immense stones have been put side by side in rows that are miles long. Sometimes the rows are arranged in order of the size of the stones, from those a few feet high to some as much as 10 feet high or more.

They look like hundreds of giants arranged in a battle formation. Some specialists think that since the stones have been arranged so simply in open fields, they indicate that the people who erected them worshiped the sun.

The meaning of these megaliths and the way in which they were built remains one of the unsolved mysteries of the world.

416

The United Kingdom

Great Britain is divided into three main regions. Scotland is to the north, Wales to the west, and England in the center and south. These three, together with Northern Ireland, make up the United Kingdom. Although these countries are united now, their people were separate tribes long ago. They spoke different languages and even today the Scottish, Irish, and Welsh people speak English differently.

There is a theory that about 250,000,000 years ago, the British Isles were attached to the European continent. Later, great movements of the earth's crust caused part of the land to sink. Seas rushed in, forming what are now

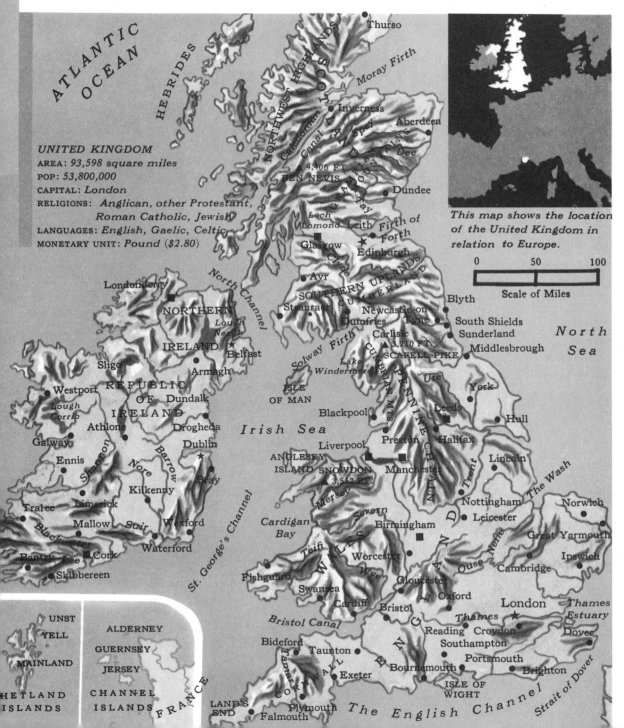

UNITED KINGDOM
AREA: *93,598 square miles*
POP: *53,800,000*
CAPITAL: *London*
RELIGIONS: *Anglican, other Protestant, Roman Catholic, Jewish*
LANGUAGES: *English, Gaelic, Celtic*
MONETARY UNIT: *Pound ($2.80)*

This map shows the location of the United Kingdom in relation to Europe.

Scale of Miles
0   50   100

called the English Channel and the North Sea. The British Isles were separated from Europe, and many small islands were formed off the coasts of Britain. The Hebrides, Orkneys, and Shetlands lie off the coast of Scotland. The Isle of Man is in the Irish Sea.

Great Britain has a mild climate. Although London lies almost 750 miles north of New York, it has no bitter winters and no long, hot summers. Warm winds from the Gulf Stream keep the weather mild all year. These winds gather moisture as they blow across the Atlantic Ocean and provide quite a bit of rain on Britain's west coast. This part of Britain has rich pasture land for the raising of cattle and sheep. Eastern Britain is drier, and the land is good for growing grain.

Great Britain has a long and rocky coastline. From Land's End, the southernmost tip of England, to Dover, there are jagged inlets and high cliffs. The Scottish coastline is also treacherous. There are often violent storms and rough seas. The North Sea coast of eastern England is quite low, with shallow waters

A typical English countryside scene, at Salisbury

and very few natural harbors. The Thames Estuary and the Wash are the only natural harbors to be found in this area of the British Isles.

Great Britain is a small country. It is only 89,295 square miles, and its rivers are therefore not very long. However, they all have large openings into the sea and deep, wide valleys through which they flow. This makes them ideal waterways for ships going from the big cities to the coast. The largest rivers are the Clyde in Scotland, the Severn in Wales and England, and the Thames in southeastern England. The Thames is the river on which London

This great industrial plant is near the coal fields of Yorkshire.

This is Land's End, at the southernmost tip of England.

The position of London on the Thames River

Snowdon Peak is a volcano in Wales.

is built. The River Mersey is on the west coast. Liverpool, the largest port after London, is on the Mersey. Other important rivers are the Trent, Tyne, Forth, Tay, Dee, and Don.

Although Great Britain is a hilly land, there are no really high mountains. The Pennines, a chain of low hills, rise in central England and run northwest to the Scottish border. The Pennines are often called the backbone of England because of the rich deposits of coal on their slopes. The Cumbrian Mountains are in northwestern England. The highest peak in England is the famous Scafell Pike. The highest peak in Great Britain is the Ben Nevis. It is in the Grampian Mountains in western Scotland.

In Cumberland, a county in northwestern England, the mountains were long ago covered by glaciers. When the climate became milder, the ice melted and filled the valleys with water. This formed the lakes of England's Lake District. The largest is Lake Windemere, which covers more than five square miles.

Scotland is the country of the highlands. In the summer the hills are covered with heather, a plant with purple blossoms. Mosses, ferns, and pine forests also cover the countryside. In Scotland, the lakes, or lochs, as they are called, lie close together. Some are connected by man-made canals that form a single waterway called the Caledonian Canal. This canal stretches completely across Scotland. The famous Loch Lomond is in this part of Great Britain.

Birmingham is the industrial center of England. The city is on a flat plain that extends from Wales to the east coast. This area is known as the Black Country because of the many coal mines and iron-ore factories.

Great Britain is very rich in mineral deposits. Tremendous veins of coal, iron ore, and clay are found in western and northern England and in southern Scotland. Some of the tin mines in Cornwall have been worked for 2,000 years, and they are still producing.

Great Britain is a country of great industry and great beauty. According to the British, two colors dominate—black and green. In the coal-mining areas black soot darkens the sky, while the English countryside is a fresh green most of the year.

Typical plants and trees of the tropics

Tropical Fruits

The tropical zone of the earth lies between the Tropic of Cancer and the Tropic of Capricorn. The equator is between these two lines. Europe and most of North America lie outside the tropics. Mexico is the only country in North America within the tropics. A large part of South America and almost all of Africa and Australia are in the tropics.

Many fruits grow in these tropical areas, which have a hot climate and frequent rainfall. The fruits come from plants and trees which need moist soil for their roots and warm air above the ground. There is an old Arab proverb about the date palm which says, "the date palm wants its feet in water and its head in the fire."

Some of the most common tropical fruits are shown in the pictures. Many of these fruits cannot be shipped long distances because they are fragile and spoil easily. So if you live very far from the tropics, you will probably see here a number of strange fruits along with the ones that are familiar to you.

The tropical zones are shown in yellow and orange.

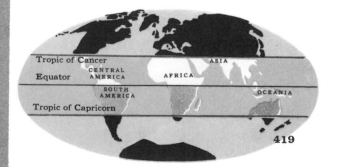

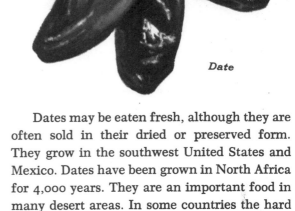

Date

Mango

Dates may be eaten fresh, although they are often sold in their dried or preserved form. They grow in the southwest United States and Mexico. Dates have been grown in North Africa for 4,000 years. They are an important food in many desert areas. In some countries the hard seed of the date is ground and used as a substitute for coffee.

Bananas are perhaps the best known tropical fruit. They are picked green, and then may be shipped many miles away, ripening on the trip. Bananas grow in great bunches from tall trees. The plants need a warm temperature and very rich soil. Bananas were known in India at the time of Alexander the Great in 300 B.C. Explorers and traders later carried them to other parts of the world. Now they are grown in all tropical countries.

Mangoes grow on very tall trees 30 to 90 feet high. The fruit itself is two to six inches long. It has thick skin and soft, juicy pulp. Mangoes resemble peaches. They are an important food in the diets of people living in the tropics. They keep well and can therefore be shipped abroad. Mangoes are one of the tropical fruits that can be purchased in the United States. They are either fresh or preserved.

Banana

Annona

Indian fig

The annona is as large as an orange. The inside is white and has a sweet taste and odor.

The pineapple is a large and well-protected fruit which grows in Hawaii, Jamaica, Brazil, and the Philippine and Canary islands. The fruit is eaten either raw or cooked, and the juice is a popular drink. Fibers from the leaves are made into cloth.

The Indian fig is a form of prickly pear grown in Mexico and also in warm regions around the Mediterranean Sea, such as Egypt, Sicily, and Spain. The fruit is eaten raw or cooked, the stems are cooked for a vegetable, and sometimes the seeds are ground into meal.

Papayas grow on trees, similar to palm trees. The fruit is large and heavy. Its size and shape is similar to a watermelon. From green papayas comes a substance called papain, which is used as a medicine to aid digestion. More papayas grow in Hawaii than any other place in the world.

Pineapple

Papaya

421

The first Estruscan cities were built on the seacoast of Italy. Gradually the Etruscans moved inland and northward into the Alps.

The Ancient Etruscan Civilization

The Etruscans are called the mysterious people. Nobody knows where they came from. All that is known is that a group of people arrived in Italy sometime around 900 or 800 B.C. and settled on the western coast. They gradu-ally moved inland, where they built many cities.

The reason so little is known about the Etruscans is that nobody can understand their written language. Although they left no books or histories, there are inscriptions in their

An Etruscan mural showing one of their gay ceremonial feasts

Nobody has deciphered Etruscan writing.

of the Etruscan art is oriental, and so many of their religious beliefs resemble the beliefs of the Egyptians, Babylonians, Assyrians, and other peoples of Asia Minor that most people nowadays think that Herodotus' account may have been close to the truth.

Although the Etruscans left no written language that can be understood, they left a great many other things which have shown scholars much about their way of life. Apparently their first cities were on the west coast of Italy, and in one of them, Vetulonia, which had been first inhabited by ancient Italians, we can find a clear record of the Etruscans' arrival. The earlier Italian tombs were quite different from those of the Etruscans. Things that had never been known in Italy, such as silver, gold, amber, and Egyptian scarabs, were found in the Etruscan tombs.

It is believed that the Etruscans may have come from Lydia, which is in modern Turkey.

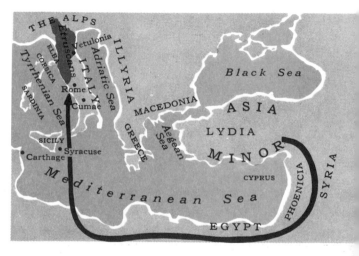

tombs and on vases and ornaments, and a great deal could be learned from these. But the scholars have not learned how to decipher them yet. The letters are much the same as the ancient Greek alphabet, but the words are not at all the same.

There is only one account of how the Etruscans came to Italy. It comes from the Greek historian Herodotus. He wrote that many years before his time, a great famine had broken out in the land of Lydia, which is where Turkey is today. The famine lasted for 18 years and, at the end of that time, the King of Lydia told his subjects that they must draw lots and divide up into two groups. One group would remain in Lydia. The other group, under the leadership of the King's son, Tyrrhenus, would set sail to find a new home. According to Herodotus, the second group stayed in many lands until it finally came to Italy, and there the people have lived ever since. He called these people the Tyrrhenians after their leader, and the sea on the west coast of Italy is known today as the Tyrrhenian Sea.

For many years scholars argued about Herodotus' statement. Many of them believed that the Etruscans were native to Italy. But so much

The tombs were elaborate. The Etruscan religion was based on an idea of life after death, much like the ideas of the Egyptians. A funeral was the occasion for a great feast and all sorts of ceremonies. When a man was buried he was buried with his weapons, his ornaments, and his household belongings.

Some tombs held models, built of stone, of complete homes. Since the Etruscans used wood to build their houses, the houses have long since rotted away, and these stone models are our only record of what the homes were like. Scholars know from the tombs that the Etruscans built their towns in terraces as the Babylonians did. We know that their homes were square but had a rounded, domelike roof, like the houses in Asia.

Historians also know a great deal about Etruscan life from the objects which have been found in the tombs. They know that they were a happy people who used bright clothing and beautiful ornaments of gold, silver, bronze, and

Etruscan lady   *Etruscan noble*

Etruscan soldier   *Etruscan commoner*

ivory. Their warriors wore helmets which were somewhat like the Grecian helmets. There was an Etruscan cavalry, and chariots were used in fighting. Many full-sized chariots were found in Etruscan tombs. There were also foot soldiers who carried spears, axes, or bows and arrows. In some of the great Etruscan battles toward the latter part of their empire, the soldiers were led by priests who carried lighted

An underground tomb built like a house

Etruscan houses were square, with dome-shaped roofs. The interiors were beautifully decorated.

The Etruscans, like the Babylonians, built cities on terraces.

torches and waved live snakes in their hands.

The Etruscan navy was a great one. For a number of centuries the Etruscans were the most powerful force in the western Mediterranean. They conquered Corsica and Sardinia and other Mediterranean islands such as Elba. After the conquest of Elba, they used its iron mines to supply their own workmen. With their powerful navy, the Etruscans were able to trade all over Asia Minor, and they imported many beautiful objects from Egypt, Greece, Cyprus, Phoenicia, and other countries across the sea.

The Etruscans also produced fine art of their own. Their statues, vases, and ornaments are all of a finer quality than those of the early Italians. They painted beautiful murals on the walls of their tombs, and their ordinary house-

Etruscan ship

hold objects were well made. All of these works of art showed a strong Asiatic influence at first. Statues of lions and fantastic beasts have been found which are very much like ones found in Assyrian ruins. Egyptian designs were found on bowls and ivory ornaments. But as the years went on, the Etruscans began to borrow more and more from the Greeks with whom they traded. A great deal of their later statuary and their vases are in the Grecian style.

The religion of the Etruscans was oriental in many ways. Their three chief gods were Tinia, Uni, and Menfra. They were a husband, wife, and daughter whom the Romans later worshiped as Jupiter, Juno, and Minerva. But the Etruscans had a great many gods of the underworld, and gods of the moon, the sun, and the dawn as well.

The priests were very important in Etruscan society. They held ceremonies in which they slaughtered a sheep or another animal in sacrifice and predicted the future from looking at the animal's liver, which is much the same custom the ancient Babylonians had. A bronze model of a liver was found in an Etruscan ruin that had the names of the Etruscan gods marked on various parts of it.

The tomb paintings show that the Etruscans had great religious festivals. They were chiefly gay ones. They had sports such as chariot races, wrestling, boxing, and dancing. They used hornlike musical instruments or two-pipe flutes in their ceremonies. The women took an equal part with the men in these sports. In fact, women seem to have played an equal part in

Etruscan goods: (1) house-shaped funeral urn which held the ashes of the dead (2) statuettes of Etruscan warriors (3) drinking vase (4) helmet

1 2 3 4

all Etruscan life, and there are many tomb statues of husband and wife sitting side by side to illustrate that married love continued forever after death.

The history of the Etruscans covers about 700 years. The first colonists, who landed on the west coast of Italy, began to move inland and build towns there. They also went northward into the Alps. Various Mediterranean islands were settled as well. For a long time they were the most important peoples in Italy. But they never had what could be called an empire, because the Etruscan cities never banded together. Each city was responsible for its own wars and conquests. The Etruscans did not fight among themselves, but they seldom got together to fight a stronger enemy.

Gradually, because of this lack of unity, the Romans, who were a rival group that was gaining in strength, began to conquer the Etruscans. The most celebrated Roman-Etruscan battle was for the city of Veii, which is near Rome. It was 10 years before the Etruscans were finally defeated, but the Romans had far fewer men and, if other Etruscans had come to Veii's assistance, the Romans could have been driven back instead.

In the same way, Etruscan sea power was finally broken by Syracuse in the battle of Cumae in 474 B.C. The Etruscans continued to have power for about 300 years after that, but it was a shrinking power. The Romans conquered more of their cities, the Samnites took others, and the Gauls captured the Etruscan possessions in the north.

By about 100 B.C. the Etruscans had become one with their conquerors, and seemingly disappeared, as mysteriously as they had come. The culture they left behind them, however, had a strong influence on the Romans. The Romans adopted many of the Etruscan ceremonies and gods. They took to divining the future from the livers of animal sacrifices. They laid out new cities as the Etruscans had. Roman magistrates wore the Etruscan purple robe and, as a sign of office, carried a bundle of sticks tied together, known as *fasces*. Etruscan trumpets were used to announce Roman ceremonies. Etruscan art, fashions, and music were copied by the Romans. The knowledge of astrology and natural science, which Etruscans had probably brought from Asia, was borrowed by the Romans. As scholars learn more and more about the mysterious Etruscans, they discover more and more of the old customs which did not die out as rapidly as the people did.

An Etruscan vase

Head of an Etruscan god

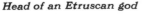

Weapons and ornaments were beautifully worked in metals such as gold, silver, and bronze.

Wagons were pulled by horses on wooden railway tracks, which were smoother than the roads of that time.

The First Steam Locomotives

During the 16th, 17th, and 18th centuries men used horse-drawn wagons to transport materials. Often, these wagons would travel on rails, and the wagon wheels would be grooved in order to stay on the rails safely. Men had found that it was easier to move a heavy load on rails, especially when there were several wagons to be moved at once.

Late in the 18th century the steam engine was invented in England by James Watt. By 1801 Richard Trevithick, another Englishman, had built the first steam locomotive. This was the first machine able to move along the ground by its own steam power. Three years later Trevithick used another locomotive to move 10 tons and 70 men in a test to show people that the locomotive could move goods easily.

Although Trevithick used his locomotive to move coal back and forth between the coal-yards and the mines, he could not persuade people to travel on this kind of transportation. In 1808 one of his locomotives was put on display in London, and passersby could see it going around in a circle. Trevithick never made much money from his idea, and he died a poor and ignored man.

Meanwhile, in 1811, John Blenkinsop developed a wheel with jagged teeth and rails with little holes for the teeth to fit into. This way there was very little danger of the wheel slipping off the rail. This invention is still used today when short railways are built on steep hills. The toothed wheel prevents the railway cars from slipping downhill.

By 1813, William Hedley had two locomotives in operation in his coal-yards. Then, in 1814, George Stephenson built his first locomotive. He was the man who really made the locomotive practical, and his engines were the first used on regular railroad lines.

In 1825, after years of construction, a railroad line was opened between Stockton and Darlington, two towns in England. The line was 38 miles long, and this was the first public railway in the world to carry passengers. George Stephenson himself drove the locomotive on the first trip, and pulled 34 wagons and about 600 passengers.

In 1829 the directors of a railway company announced a contest among all the locomotive builders. The directors wanted to find a locomotive that would meet certain technical requirements, and the winner would be used on their new railroad, which was to run between the cities of Liverpool and Manchester.

Although 10 builders entered, only five showed up for the contest. After seven days of tests, George Stephenson's *Rocket* was proclaimed the winner. He was able to go 12 miles an hour with a heavy load and a few passengers. Although this was no faster than a man could go on a bicycle, the locomotive could carry thousands of pounds of materials and hundreds of people.

In 1830, after six years of work, the 31-mile-long railroad between Liverpool and Manchester was finally finished. Under the direction of

Richard Trevithick's locomotive was exhibited in London in 1808.

George Stephenson, more than 60 bridges had been built to support tracks, and the first railway tunnel had been dug out.

On September 15, the opening ceremonies were held. There were two tracks along the route. On one of them George Stephenson drove his most powerful locomotive, the *Northumbrian*. On the other track, seven other locomotives would make the same trip. These machines pulled railroad cars which carried government officials, foreign ministers, and important persons of the time. It was a big occasion, and the cars for guests were beautifully decorated. The car in which the Prime Minister of England rode was covered with a red canopy supported by elegant columns.

The route had been checked along every foot of the way, just in case a careless workman had left one of his tools on the track. The locomotives worked perfectly. In the *Northumbrian*, Stephenson would show off by letting the

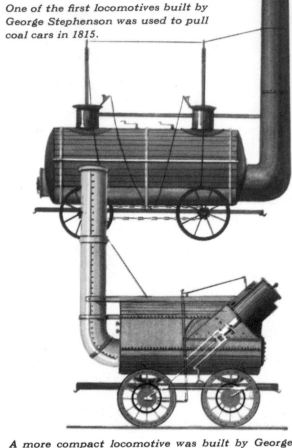

One of the first locomotives built by George Stephenson was used to pull coal cars in 1815.

The oldest locomotive still in existence was built by William Hedley in 1813 and was used for more than 50 years.

A more compact locomotive was built by George Stephenson's son, Robert, in 1828.

The Rocket *was the engine which won the seven-day locomotive contest of 1829.*

other engines pass him, and then putting on a burst of speed to catch up.

When the party arrived at a station along the route, one of the locomotives was used to demonstrate how easily such a big machine could be controlled. It moved forwards and backwards, to show that it could work in re-

The festive opening ceremonies of the Liverpool-Manchester railroad took place in 1830.

verse. There is a story that one of the officials, accustomed to trains that only moved forward, stood behind the locomotive. Before he could move away, he was knocked down and injured.

It seemed that everything was lost, just when success was in sight. For years people had refused to take steam locomotion seriously. Now, just when the locomotive was being used on an important railroad, this accident would scare people away from using railroads for many more years.

Suddenly, Stephenson had an idea. "Put the man on the *Northumbrian*," he said. "I'll take him to Manchester."

It had not occurred to anyone that a train could be used in this urgent and practical way. The man was put on board, and he was carried to a hospital more comfortably and quickly than he could have been carried by any other vehicle of that time.

The Liverpool-Manchester railroad was the first railway on which steam locomotion was used as the only means of transport. On previous railways, some of the power was still supplied by horses. But from that time on, railroad

transportation was quickly accepted by people throughout the world.

In the United States, an inventor named Oliver Evans built a steam engine as early as 1804. But he could not interest people in steam locomotion as a regular means of transportation. Locomotives seemed too dangerous, and most travel was by canals between cities.

John Stevens was given the first American charter to build a railroad in 1815. He is called the father of the railroad. Stevens had a great deal of trouble when he tried to get money and help when it was time to start construction.

An American company bought a locomotive from Robert Stephenson, son of George Stephenson, in 1828. By 1830 the first steam railroad was in operation in the United States. Finally, in 1869, the first railroad tracks across the whole United States were completed.

The story of steam locomotion is the story of many men. They already had tracks and the power of steam engines. Each man used the discoveries of the men before to develop a practical and economical steam motor on wheels that could move itself along tracks.

How Man Uses Water

Man cannot live without water. Water covers nearly three quarters of the earth's surface and forms almost three quarters of the human body. Water is found in three states—solid, liquid, and gas. At temperatures below 32 degrees Fahrenheit, water becomes solid. It is a gas at temperatures above 212 degrees Fahrenheit. Water as a solid is found in ice and hail, in snowfields and glaciers. Water as a gas or vapor is invisible in the air around us.

As the sun shines down on the earth, it heats the seas and oceans and causes the water on the surface to evaporate. The same process of evaporation occurs when a pot of water is boiled. If the water is boiled long enough, it will disappear as steam or vapor. Every day millions of tons of water evaporate from the oceans.

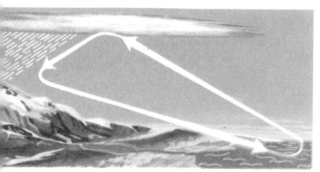

Three forms of water—gaseous clouds, solid glaciers, and liquid oceans

Water is also added to the atmosphere by the breathing process of plants and animals. They exhale water vapor with their breath. A large elm tree, for example, may give off over 300 quarts of water as vapor in one day.

Through the process of evaporation, tremendous amounts of water continually rise from the earth to form clouds. The higher the temperature of the air, the more water it can hold in the form of vapor. If the air is cooled and contains enough vapor, the vapor condenses into minute liquid droplets which form around tiny particles of dust. In the upper air the result is clouds. Lower down, it is fog or mist.

Further cooling of the air causes the tiny cloud droplets to combine into drops so big

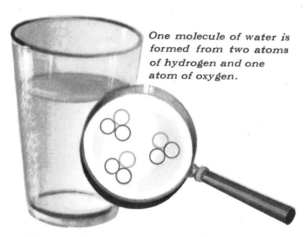

One molecule of water is formed from two atoms of hydrogen and one atom of oxygen.

and heavy that they fall back to the earth as rain. If the temperature is below freezing, the cloud will consist of ice crystals rather than drops of water, and instead of rain there will be snow. Scientists estimate that it takes about 8,000,000 particles of water vapor in a cloud to form one drop of rain.

After snow, hail, or sleet hits the earth, it eventually melts into liquid water. Then, like rainwater, it evaporates again into the atmosphere or soaks into the ground.

Water that goes into the ground may be absorbed immediately by plant roots. Some water that goes beneath the earth's surface runs downward until it reaches a rock layer that it cannot penetrate, at which point the water runs along the rock shelves according to the slope. It may run for hundreds of miles in underground rivers before ever reaching the surface again. There are deeply buried lakes, too. Some underground water rises up to form springs which feed lakes, ponds, and streams on the surface of the earth.

The surface waters of the earth flow from tiny springs and mountain ponds, down streams and brooks, over cataracts and falls, through whirlpools and eddies, all heading for the lowest level they can reach. Great arteries of watersheds are formed on all the land continents. Watersheds are divisions which separate the drainage basin of one river system from another. They feed into the great lakes and rivers that eventually empty into the seas and oceans.

HOW MAN USES WATER

Water has played a large part in forming and controlling human life. Scientists believe that all life started in the oceans. And all plants and animals need water to drink. Without water all living things would die.

Primitive man used water for drinking, for cleaning himself, and for transportation. The most ancient civilizations developed alongside bodies of water because the water was needed for the crops and as a means of transportation. Man built boats to navigate the seas and rivers. He learned to catch fish to eat.

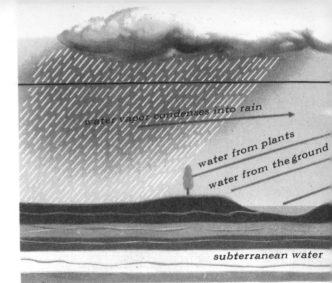

water vapor condenses into rain

water from plants

water from the ground

subterranean water

Water is needed by all animals.

At first man used water only for drinking.

The Mediterranean Sea saw the rise of many cultures along its shores—Phoenician, Egyptian, Cretan, Greek, and Roman. The Phoenicians were the first to develop trade on the coasts of the Mediterranean Sea.

Another nautical people were the Vikings. They explored most of the North Atlantic Ocean in their sturdy ships, reaching the North American continent as well as the shores of western Europe.

Some of the greatest and wealthiest nations in history have been those who mastered the seas. The Cretans, Greeks, and Romans developed great civilizations by dominating the Mediterranean Sea. In more modern times, the British Empire was built and maintained by vast naval power throughout the world. Today the

Man learned to bathe in water.

Primitive man probably made the first boat from a log he found floating in a stream.

Water is used for agricultural irrigation.

Water is used to power a grist mill.

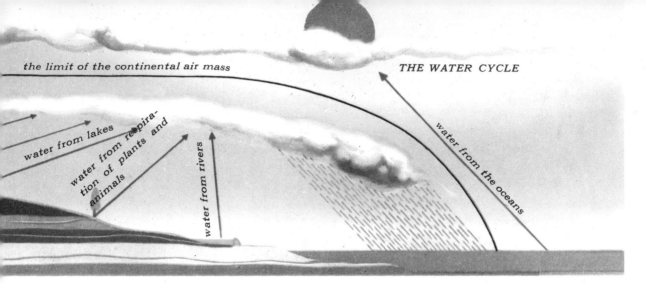

the limit of the continental air mass

THE WATER CYCLE

water from lakes

water from respiration of plants and animals

water from rivers

water from the oceans

A variety of containers used for holding water

ancient water jug called an amphora

canteen

pitcher

chemical flask

glass goblet

basin

washtub

United States is the wealthiest nation on earth with the greatest international trade. This tremendous commerce is handled by the largest merchant fleet in the world.

Rivers, too, have been important in human destiny. The great Babylonian civilization grew up around the Tigris and Euphrates rivers. The Egyptians built their cities along the Nile. Most of the important cities of the world are built near rivers. London in England, Paris in France, Rome in Italy, and New York, St. Louis, and New Orleans in the United States are all on major rivers.

Water, whether fresh from the land or salt from the sea, is made up of two basic elements —hydrogen and oxygen. A molecule of water has two atoms of hydrogen and one atom of oxygen. Only water made in the laboratory is ever really pure. Natural water always has some other mineral substance dissolved in it.

A cross-section of earth shows subterranean water gushing from a spring.

433

HOW MAN USES WATER

Water is called hard when it contains large amounts of minerals, such as iron and sulfur. Hard water has magnesium and calcium salts, too, while soft water contains few salts. If a pot of water is boiled until all the water has evaporated, dustlike particles are left in the pot. These are the mineral salts that were in the water.

By distilling water in the laboratory, the chemist can get pure water. He boils it and collects the water vapor in a flask. As the water vapor cools, it becomes liquid again. The impurities are collected as a residue because they vaporize at different temperatures than the hydrogen and oxygen in pure water.

Hard water or mineral water is good for drinking because of its healthful elements. It does not lather well, so it is poor for washing. Soft water makes wonderful suds, but it is not so good to drink.

Man has learned to control and use water for hundreds of things. Dams have been built

Some of the many uses of water
(1) drinking (2) cooking (3) washing (4) bathing (5) laundry (6) heating (7) watering gardens (8) watering livestock (9) irrigating land (10) operating gristmills (11) fountains (12) operating industrial plants (13) hydroelectric power (14) travel (15) railroad steam engines (16) swimming pools

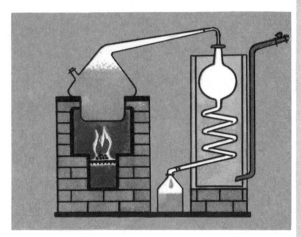
In the laboratory, pure water is obtainable through the process of distillation.

Rivers— Starting Points of Civilization

All the early civilizations grew up along the banks and mouths of rivers. The Chinese first lived along the banks of the Yangtze River, and the Ganges River was the site of the early settlements in India. Egypt grew up along the Nile, and the Babylonian Empire flourished between the Tigris and the Euphrates rivers.

The land on either side of a river usually is fertile enough for farming. This was particularly important for the early eastern civilizations which developed in hot, dry lands.

Transportation is simplified if there is a waterway nearby. And it is possible to take merchandise to central places via waterways. Places where several branches join the main stream of the river are natural crossroads. They often become the sites of cities.

River water is used for drinking. Fish in rivers provide food. As man learned to use the forces of nature, water power became an important source of energy. Long ago, water wheels were built to provide energy. Now, giant factories use electricity that has been created by water power.

(1) Rivers originate high in the mountains. Rainfall and melting snow and ice travel down the mountainsides. When several streams join together, a river channel is formed.

(2) Dams are built across rivers, partly to form reservoirs and slow down the flow of the river. By damming the river, man can use the water to advantage. Irrigation and flood control are possible. At the present time, one of the most important functions of dams is to transform the power of the water into electric power. The power can be used to run factories and light up cities.

(3) Land that does not get enough rainfall can be watered by rivers. The water is diverted to be evenly distributed over dry farm lands.

to control rivers and conserve water. Great hydroelectric plants provide electric power for home and industry. Aqueducts carry water from one place to another. Canals give easier and cheaper transportation, and great irrigation projects have changed deserts into productive land. Wells, reservoirs, cisterns, and pools are made to conserve water. Man-made lakes have been constructed and rivers rerouted to control water and to use it better.

Water is also one of man's greatest sources of recreation. Fishing, boating, and swimming are popular sports.

Water is vital to life in the city. It is piped under streets and pumped up throughout the tallest skyscrapers. Hydrants provide water under pressure for fire protection, and fountains are used to beautify gardens and parks.

The study of water is divided into several fields. Hydraulics is the study of moving water and how to use it. Hydrography is the science of the water of the earth—the geography of the rivers, lakes, and oceans. Hydrology is concerned with the medicinal qualities of mineral water, while hydrotherapy deals with the treatment of human diseases through baths of various sorts. Hydrometry is the study of the speed and levels of flowing water, and hygrometry is the study of humidity, the amount of moisture in the atmosphere.

From whatever source water comes, from the seas and oceans, from lakes and streams, or from the sky in the form of rain and snow, it is the greatest of man's natural resources.

A panoramic view of some of the important places found on a river

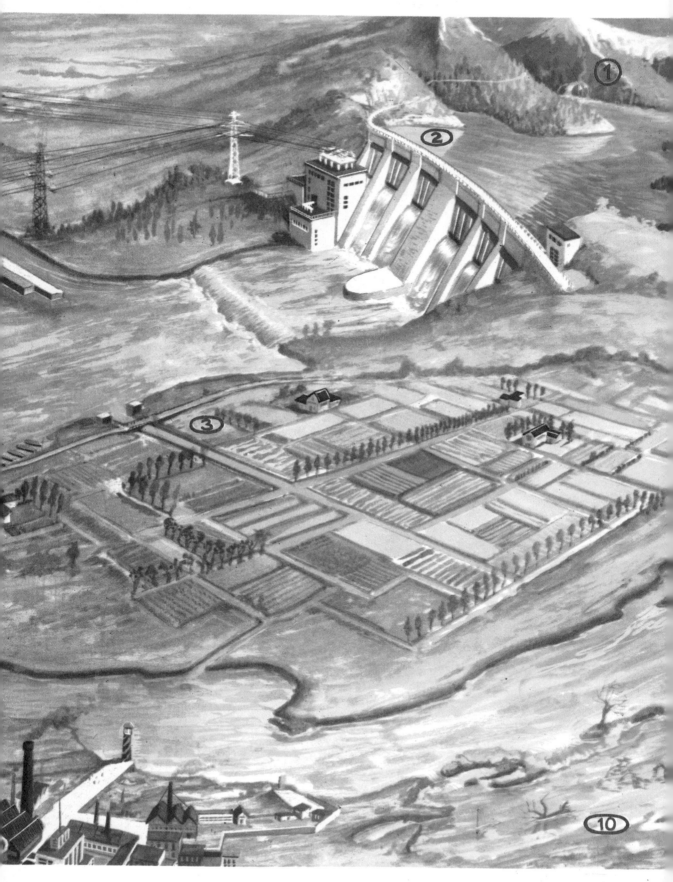

435

(4) In some cities river water is used for drinking. It must first be purified, so that it will be safe to drink. Then it is stored in reservoirs.

(5) Waste products from factories are frequently dumped into rivers. This is an inexpensive way of disposing of refuse, but it often destroys fish and contaminates the water downstream. The practice is being discontinued.

(6) If a river is navigable, it is used to transport goods and people. Travel on water is slower than on land, but it is cheaper. Great commercial empires have been built along navigable rivers such as the Rhine, and in some places, almost all travel is by riverboat.

(7) A river provides many jobs. Some people are fishermen, some run boats, some search for minerals in river beds, and others dredge up gravel from the river bottoms.

(8) Sometimes, as a river reaches the sea, it forms an inlet. If the inlet is deep and sheltered from the waves of the sea and the river current, it forms a harbor. Many commercially important cities have been built where there were large harbors. New York, Bombay, Rotterdam, and Buenos Aires are such cities.

(9) A river carries with it thousands of tons of sediment and crushed rocks as it travels toward the sea. Some of this material settles to the bottom of the river. Some of it overflows the banks when the river rises. Sometimes this material is deposited at the mouth of a river. Over the years the sediment forms triangular islands, called deltas. The delta of the Nile is the most famous of these rich deposits.

(10) If mountain snow melts too quickly, or if there are heavy rainfalls, the added water causes rivers to overflow their banks. A sudden flood is a disaster to the people whose land is covered by water. But in some cases, when a river such as the Nile overflows, the farmers benefit by the watering of their land and the rich surface soil that is left when the floodwaters recede.

In earliest times, water travel was the best means of exchanging goods and ideas between different peoples. Modern means of transport and communication have changed this. But rivers are still important and have a great influence on the growth of nations.

The Plow

One of the first implements of civilization was the plow. After the plow was invented to cultivate the soil, man could live in one place instead of wandering around to find food.

The first plowing seems to have been done along the Nile in Egypt or the Euphrates in Mesopotamia. The oldest ruins of agricultural settlements have been found by scientists in these river valleys.

The ancient plow only loosened and stirred the soil. Modern plows slice down deep into the earth and turn it over bringing the rich bottom soil upward. The sod is covered by fresh soil in which seed is planted. The turned-under sod provides space under the soil for air and water. It also rots and provides nourishment for the crop growing over it.

After the walking plow came the sulky—a horsedrawn plow that could be ridden. Next came the gang plow. This also can be ridden, and it has two or more moldboards to lift, turn, and chop up the soil. Tractors have taken the

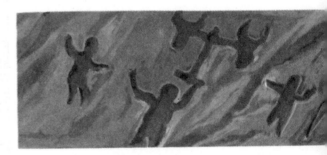

These two ancient pictures were found scratched on a rock in a Swedish farm district. Above are three men, and a plow drawn by oxen represented only by the shapes of their heads. Below, a plowman of very early times holds in one hand a stick to drive his animals. In the other hand he has a bag, which probably contains seeds.

Prehistoric man made his hook-shaped plow from the forked branch of a tree. He dragged it himself.

The wooden plow of the Greeks and early Latins was more complicated. It was pulled by oxen.

The Egyptians had many slaves and they were used to pull the plows.

The Romans made great improvements in the plow. They made the share of metal, and two wheels were added to give the plow extra balance.

This type of plow has been used almost unchanged until today.

place of horses on big farms and on level land. But in many underdeveloped places, wooden walking plows with iron-tipped shares—and even hand plows—are still in use.

When the sod is turned under, it makes a space for air and water under the top layer of soil.

PARTS OF A HORSE-DRAWN PLOW

This kind of plow has a coulter (1) that makes a vertical cut in the sod. It cuts clean, sharp furrows. The share (2) is a strong steel blade that cuts into the soil horizontally. The moldboard (3) is a curved surface which turns over and breaks up the slice of soil cut by the coulter and the share. The beam (4) is the part by which the plow is drawn. It is usually iron or steel. The handles (5) allow the plowman to control the plow. The clevis, or bridle (6), to which the animals are attached, has on it a device which allows the plowman to regulate the width and depth of the turned sod. The landslide (7) is an iron or steel sidepiece opposite the moldboard. It presses against the ground to offset the pressure against the moldboard and steadies the motion of the plow.

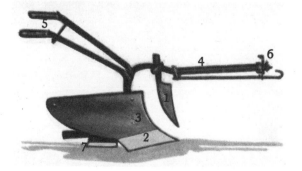

Circuses

The ancient Greeks staged chariot races, and wild animals performed for the Pharaohs of Egypt. From the earliest times, all civilized societies have been entertained by jugglers, acrobats, and clowns. But the first people to create anything like the modern circus were the Romans, who made it a major spectacle.

The Circus Maximus in Rome was the earliest Roman circus and the biggest. It could seat 150,000 people. They mainly watched chariot racing, but there were also foot races, wrestling, boxing, acrobats, and trained animal acts.

Many statues were made of the Roman chariots. Some of them still adorn public buildings in Europe.

A golden statue of a charioteer

The Roman people enjoyed it so much that some critics claimed that they would never object to misrule of any kind as long as they were given their ration of "bread and circuses."

Circuses included such athletic events as foot races, boxing, and wrestling. There were also tightrope walkers and tamed animals such as those in the circuses of today. But the main event in Roman circuses of that time was chariot racing.

The Latin word *circus* meant a chariot race and also the arena in which the race was held. The first and largest of these was the Circus Maximus, which was laid out in the third century before Christ and developed into a huge U-shaped stadium that could seat 150,000

The Colosseum in Rome as it looked in ancient times. In it gladiators fought wild beasts and each other to satisfy bloodthirsty crowds.

441

When a chariot was wrecked on a turn, the charioteer had to try to avoid the deadly hooves of the other horses.

people. The central racing area was covered with sand. It was divided by a low wall running down the middle, called the *spina*. The chariots, drawn by two or four or more horses, had to circle the *spina* seven times during a race. The sport was very dangerous. The charioteers, who were usually slaves, received large sums for winning races. One slave, Crescentius, managed to save more than a million and a half *sesterces*—about 150,000 dollars—by the time he was 22. But he was one of the lucky ones. Many of his friends and opponents were dead, having been killed in the accidents that often occurred as the chariots rounded the turns.

Chariot races were mild compared to the spectacles presented in the amphitheaters. The biggest of these was the Colosseum in Rome. Unlike the circus, the amphitheater was not free. Customers bought tickets to see animals fight each other, gladiators fight animals, and gladiators fight among themselves. Most gladiators were slaves, but a few were impoverished freemen who were willing to bet their lives on the slim chance of gaining fame and fortune.

The main attraction of the amphitheater was death. Animals tore each other to pieces. Gladiators showed no mercy if the crowd turned thumbs down—the sign that a defeated opponent should be killed. Under the early Ro-

man emperors, thousands of Christians were thrown to wild beasts which had been starved and hungered for food. The spectacles often ended with a hunt, in which scores or hundreds of animals were cornered and slaughtered by armed men. These were so popular that some species of animals were nearly wiped out in order to supply the Roman people with entertainment.

Under Emperor Constantine, who became a Christian, the practice of throwing condemned criminals to wild beasts was outlawed. In A.D. 404, battles among gladiators were made illegal. The last wild animal hunt was held about 100 years later. The Barbarians, who sacked Rome, did not have the same taste for blood, and the Circus Maximus and the Colosseum fell into disrepair. Nothing is left of the Circus except a pile of stones, and the remains of the Colosseum have become a symbol of Rome.

The milder parts of the circus did not stop when the Roman spectacles did. Tumblers, acrobats, jugglers, and clowns continued to entertain the people of the Middle Ages, but large circuses vanished until the 18th century.

In about 1750, various groups of animal trainers and trick riders organized shows which began to tour England and Europe. They came to America about 50 years later. The circus was

Clowns can do many different acts and make them look easy and funny (1). Kangaroos hold boxing matches (2). A bareback rider becomes almost a part of his mount. It takes years to train a circus horse (3). Acrobats do difficult handstands (4). Elephants are the main attraction of most modern circuses (5). Jugglers never drop a tenpin except on purpose (6). The human cannonball is shot across the ring (7). Trapeze acts look effortless, but are among the most dangerous performances (8). Seals can balance almost anything on their noses (9). Chimpanzees are dressed like sailors and they ride bicycles (10). Even the hippopotamus wears a costume (11). The knife thrower always misses the pretty girl (12). Bears are able to ride unicycles (13). More than a hundred lion trainers have been killed in this kind of act since 1820, when it began (14). Audiences are always fascinated by the skills of snake charmers (15).

reborn, but in a milder form. Horses were the stars of these new shows, and bareback riders who do acrobatics on moving horses are still the main attraction of many modern circuses.

The first modern circuses were small, but as time went on, they merged with one another and grew bigger. In Europe they were so popular in the 19th century that large, permanent buildings were erected in the major cities so that circuses could play all winter long. In America, circuses usually rested during the winter and traveled in summer. All the animals, performers, and equipment were transported first on wagons, then in railroad cars, and now in trailer trucks. They toured from town to town, giving two performances—one in the afternoon, another in the evening.

The Big Top is the main tent of a traveling circus. It is set up each morning and taken down after the last show of the evening. Then it is loaded on trucks and carried to the next town.

This meant that the entire circus had to be set up each morning and taken down each night after the last show. This activity was one of the most exciting parts of circus life. The wagons arrived at the chosen place, usually a field outside of town, long before dawn. Everybody helped to put up the big tents. The elephants were trained to help in this work. After breakfast, the performers had an hour's sleep and then dressed for the parade, which was an important part of the circus. The wagons were gaily painted, the horses were curried and brushed until their coats shone, and the performers wore bright costumes that glittered in the morning sun. With flags flying and bands playing, the parade would pass through the main street so that everybody would know the circus had come to town.

After lunch the children's performance was held. The clowns had a big part in this, and the jugglers, acrobats, and animal trainers did their simplest acts. In the evening, at the main performance, everyone did his best for the adults. Throughout the show, vendors circulated among the crowd selling peanuts, jelly apples, and "circus candy." During the intermission, the audience flocked to see the freaks in the sideshows. Many people remember with fondness the smell of sawdust, which was, and still is, a sign of the circus. Many people remember, too, the desire to run away with the circus. Actually many children did this, and still do, for being a part of a circus seems very exciting to people who live ordinary lives.

As time went on, circuses got bigger and bigger, until finally there were only two major circuses in the United States. They were Ringling Brothers, and Barnum and Bailey. Shortly after 1900, these two circuses combined to create the largest and most splendid circus that has existed since Roman times. One hundred railroad cars were needed to transport it. It carried a main tent seating 12,000 persons. There were as many as 50 elephants, scores of other animals, and several hundred performers. Altogether, this great circus employed more than 1,000 people, all of whom traveled with "The Greatest Show on Earth" each summer.

Circuses are smaller than they once were, and they usually don't travel so far. Nevertheless, they are still around, and the acrobats, jugglers, performing animals, trapeze artists, bareback riders, and clowns are just as exciting to watch as they ever were. Some people are afraid that the circus is dying in the United States. They think that television and movies have taken its place. But the circus will always exist as long as children want to see it.

TIME CHART
VOLUME 5

represents all time from the beginning of the earth to the present, which is calculated by most authorities to be four to six billion years. The lowest band covers a period of 1,000 years, counting back from the present to A.D. 1000. The band above it covers 4,000 years, counting back from the year A.D. 1000 to 5,000 years ago. Each band represents about four times as many years as the band directly below it. The third band covers 16,000 years, the one above it 64,000 years, and so on. As you go back in time, dates become more and more uncertain. Dates before recorded history—about 3000 B.C.—are the calculations and expert guesses of archeologists and geologists.

Oceans form and cool enough for first life

4,000,000,000 TO 6,000,000,000 YEARS AGO

One-celled animals and plants   Land plants

Beginning and end of the dinosaurs

Age of Mammals

1,000,000,000
3 OR MORE GLACIAL ERAS EACH
350,000,000 LASTING
100,000,000 ABOUT ONE MILLION
20,000,000 YEARS

5,000,000

Early man makes his first fire and first implements

1,250,000

350,000   LAST GLACIAL ERA

Development of Stone Age man

90,000

Cave paintings and pictures carved on bone tools

20,000

Ur, first city, has gold and copper

Plow used in Asia and Egypt, p. 438   Stone monuments built, p. 415   Egyptian pyramids

5,000 YEARS AGO
= 3000 B.C.

Indo-Europeans migrate to western Europe, p. 394   2000 B.C.

Phoenicians migrate to Europe, p. 394

Height of Greek civilization   1000 B.C.   Circus Maximus built in Rome, p. 440

Birth of Christ   A.D. 1 B.C.   Height of Roman civilization   Aristotle, p. 366

A.D. 1000   Huns invade Europe, p. 394   Moslems migrate to Europe, p. 394

First medical university in Europe, p. 398

DARK AGES

1097   First Crusade

Genghis Khan   1206

1300   First gunpowder

Joan of Arc burned at the stake, p. 403   1460   First printing, first type   Siege of Orleans, p. 403   RENAISSANCE

Martin Luther writes 95 theses, p. 396   Columbus   1492   Aztecs conquered by Cortes, p. 408

Abel Tasman lands in Tasmania, p. 371

1698   First steam engine

Captain Cook discovers New Zealand, p. 371

First practical steam locomotive, p. 427   Mexico wins independence from Spain, p. 408

Joan of Arc made a saint, p. 403

Wright Brothers'—first flight, p. 363   Atomic energy   1942

A.D. 2000

The type in red with page numbers (such as p. 403) refers to Titles and facts in this volume. Items in black are chosen from the complete chronology in Volume 16 to help place events.

EACH BAND COVERS FOUR TIMES AS MANY YEARS AS THE BAND BELOW IT

16,000 YEARS   4,000 YEARS   1,000 YEARS

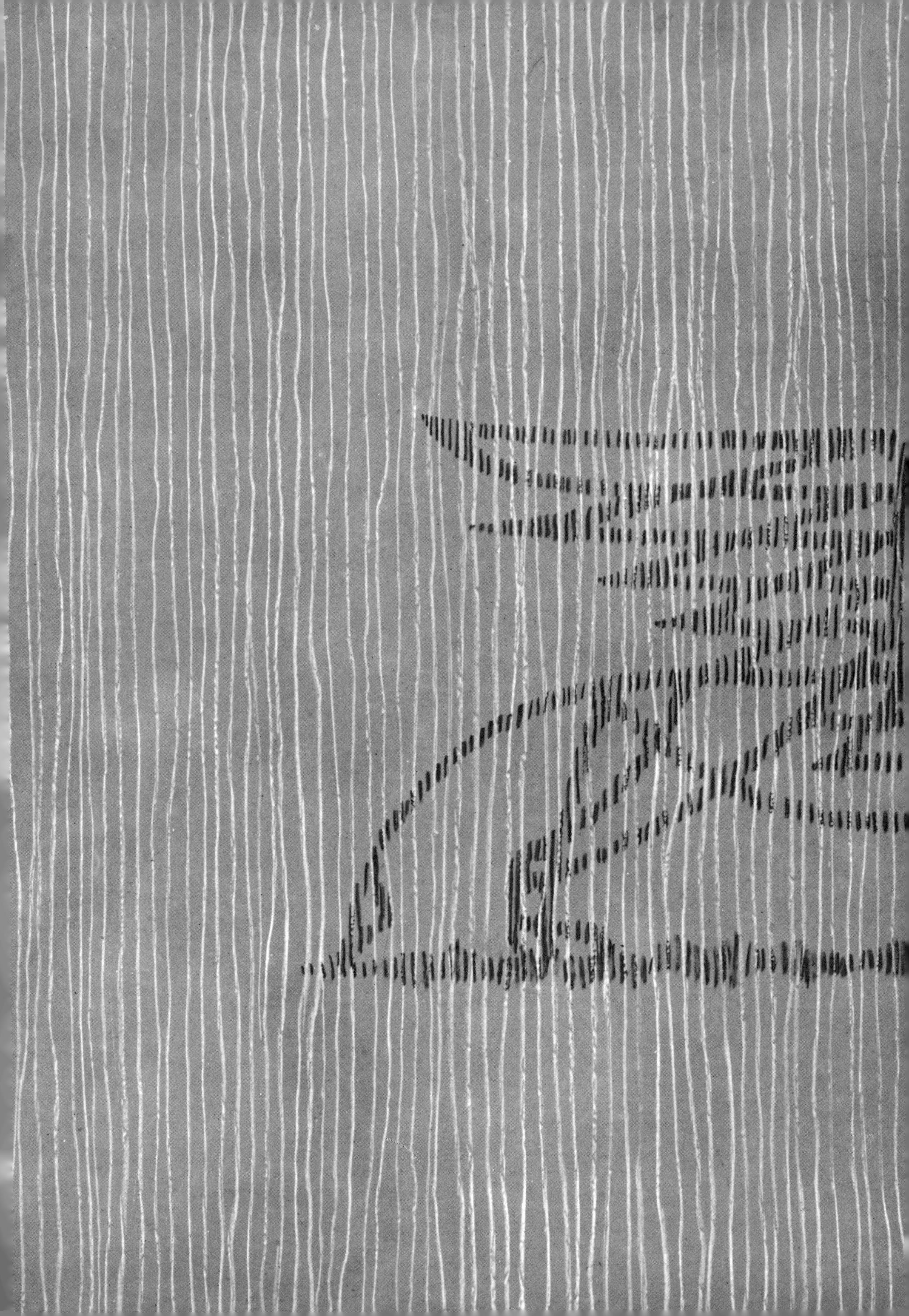